MAKE or BREAK
your church
in 365 days

"Read this book and improve your competence and credibility in ministry."
—Dr. John Jackson, Ph.D., President, William Jessup University

"Paul Borden has extensive experience in breathing new life into congregations and whole denominations. If you are interested in effective fruitfulness as well as faithfulness, read every word in this very practical book. Then implement it."
—Dr. Stuart Robinson, Founding Pastor, Crossway Baptist Church, Melbourne, Australia

"Paul Borden has written several good books. This book, however, is a great book. Why? First, this book feels like Paul is literally sitting with you face to face in a seminar room. It is engaging, invites dialogue, and provides the kind of coaching that a pastor in any stage of experience needs. Second, this book establishes a "base line" for personal evaluation. Everyone knows that church transformation is messy. What is needed is the ability to compare your reality as a leader to the normative experience of successful pastors. Third, this book is practical, not just because of the tips to that are offered, but because of the standard of accountability that is provided. Finally, this book gets you started on the right foot. Transformation can take five to seven years to accomplish, but this book gives you vital

information on what to do in the very first year. Success for the long haul depends on the first step. This is the first step."
—Tom Bandy, church development expert and author

"This hard-to-put-down book comes as close to providing a personal coach as the printed page can offer. I've never seen an approach like this 'one year' book. If I had read it in seminary or during one of my early pastorates, I'm certain I would have been a lot more effective both as pastor and leader."
—Warren Bird, Author and Research Director, Leadership Network

"Paul Borden's love for churches and the pastors who lead them, his passion for helping leaders serve effectively, and his vast ministry knowledge accumulated through his years of consulting all converge in this book. *Make or Break Your Church in 365 Days* is a game changer!"
—Bill Hoyt, NexStep Coaching and Consulting

"Finally, we have a book for pastors that gives practical advice that makes sense when you are starting out in a new ministry position. I will be handing this book out to all of my staff and colleagues who are starting out new ministry positions."
—Greg Alderman, Senior Pastor, Christ Community Church, Carmichael, California

"Motivational and eminently practical, this volume addresses most of the common contemporary struggles of pastors who seek to lead from a biblically missional perspective."
—Martin Crain, Director of Professional Doctoral Programs, Associate Professor of Pastoral Theology, Trinity Evangelical Divinity School

"Paul Borden knows more about transformational church leadership than anyone else I know. In these pages, he cooks it down to a detailed agenda for how to manage one's time and leadership in the critical first year as pastor of a congregation. I wish I had something like this when I graduated seminary. Too many of us muddle our way through, spending too many years figuring it out when there are proven ways to turn churches around. Start here!"
--Paul Nixon, church consultant and author

PAUL D. BORDEN

MAKE or BREAK
your church
in 365 days

A daily guide to leading
effective change

ABINGDON PRESS

Nashville

MAKE OR BREAK YOUR CHURCH IN 365 DAYS

A DAILY GUIDE TO LEADING EFFECTIVE CHANGE

Copyright © 2012 by Abingdon Press

This book is printed on acid-free paper.

Library of Congress Cataloging-in-Publication Data

Borden, Paul D.
   Make or break your church in 365 days : a daily guide to leading effective change / Paul D. Borden.
      p.   cm.
   ISBN 978-1-4267-4502-7 (book - pbk. / trade pbk. : alk. paper)   1. Pastoral theology.   2. Church management.   3. Christian leadership.   4. Church renewal.   5. Change (Psychology)—Religious aspects—Christianity.   I. Title.
   BV4011.3.B67 2012
   254—dc23
                                                                                            2011045073

12 13 14 15 16 17 18 19 20 21—10 9 8 7 6 5 4 3 2 1
MANUFACTURED IN THE UNITED STATES OF AMERICA

To All the Pastors and Planters,
along with their spouses and families, who have led and are
currently leading effective, healthy, growing congregations. Lead-
ing systemic change and starting healthy reproducing congrega-
tions require hard work regardless of one's talents or gift mix.
You who have done well and you who continue to serve with dis-
tinction: congratulations! Also, to those of you in this group who
allowed me to interview you, thank you for your time and your
contribution to the kingdom work of God.

Teresa Flint-Borden
You have been the first editor of every book I have written. Your
additions, subtractions, and comments have added immensely to
anything I have created. You do the same for me in life. Thank
you for your wisdom and insight. You make me better at all that I
do. You are God's treasure to me. I love you.

CONTENTS

CHAPTER 1: INTRODUCTION.. 11

Leadership: Credibility and Competence 13

Purpose 16

Assumptions... 16

Parameters: You Must Start Somewhere 26

The Template: Getting from Here to There 28

Conclusion 29

CHAPTER 2: IS MISSION POSSIBLE REALLY MISSION
    IMPOSSIBLE?.. 31

The Fundamental Question.. 33

A Rest and Recuperation Church 36

A Missional Church 38

Conclusion 47

CHAPTER 3: 365 DAYS AND COUNTING 49

Conclusion 71

CHAPTER 4: MONDAY: TRANSITION DAY............................. 73

Introduction... 74

Before the Office Opens: Beginning Ministry
    at Breakfast 76

Monday Morning: Finishing Up Sunday's Work.......................... 78

Monday Afternoon: Organization and
    Planning 86

Monday Evening 89

Conclusion 90

CHAPTER 5: TUESDAY: PREPARATION DAY........................ 93

Introduction.. 94

Assumptions.. 96

Tuesday Morning: Study... 98

Tuesday Lunch: Civic Connections 105

Tuesday Aftenoon: Preparation.................................... 105

Tuesday Evening 106

Conclusion 109

CHAPTER 6: WEDNESDAY: COMMUNITY DAY.................. 111

Introduction.. 112

Wednesday Morning: Six Months of
Preparation for Wednesdays 116

A Special Lunch 122

Wednesday Afternoon 123

A Major Warning 125

Conclusion 127

CHAPTER 7: THURSDAY: FINALIZATION DAY.................. 129

Introduction.. 130

The Use of Narrative in Preaching
Inductively.. 132

Thursday Morning: Seven A.M. until Lunch 140

Thursday Afternoon.. 143

Conclusion 145

CHAPTER 8: FRIDAY: BOUNDARY DAY 147

The Nature of This Chapter 148

Establishing Boundaries before You Arrive................ 149

The Pastor's Boundaries... 151

Recreating 153

Family Life 155

Smaller Congregations and Younger
  Families 157

Partnerships, Not Team 158

Friendships 159

Self-Learning 161

Being in the Community 162

Conclusion 163

CHAPTER 9: SATURDAY: ANTICIPATION DAY 165

Six Thirty to Eight Thirty A.M. 166

Nine to Eleven A.M. 170

Eleven A.M. to Twelve Thirty P.M. 172

Twelve Thirty to Three P.M. 173

Three to Five Thirty P.M. 173

The Rest of the Day 178

Conclusion 178

CHAPTER 10: SUNDAY: CELEBRATION DAY 181

Early Morning 182

Midmorning 185

The Worship Service (Before the Sermon) 189

The Sermon 192

Lunch Meeting after the Worship Service 193

Sunday Afternoon 196

Late Afternoon and Evening 197

Conclusion 197

APPENDIX ONE: COMMON LEADERSHIP ISSUES 201

APPENDIX TWO: MEAL MEETINGS, MONEY,
  AND WAISTLINES 213

CHAPTER 1

INTRODUCTION

Pastor Fred sat in his office on his first Monday morning as pastor of First Church. He, his spouse, and their two young children were settling in as he prepared to start his third professional ministry responsibility. They had already experienced the welcome dinner with many from the congregation in attendance. After preaching his first sermon yesterday, he and his family stood at the back of the church meeting and greeting many people from the congregation. Already some people were sharing their expectations for him. Some invited him over for a meal in the near future, others let him know of shut-ins who would like to meet the new pastor, and others hoped he would soon share his office hours so they could meet with him. A few even broached ministry areas with needs to be addressed soon.

This would be his second experience as a lead pastor. Upon graduating from seminary, he served two years as a youth pastor in a congregation that averaged just fewer than two hundred in attendance. He was responsible for both the junior and the senior high students. He felt he did a competent job of ministering to the young people. But he wasn't cut out to be a youth pastor. He saw little spiritual growth and no numerical growth in the youth department.

After the youth ministry, Fred became the solo pastor of a smaller congregation that averaged sixty each Sunday. He served there three years and initiated some growth so that the congregation averaged about seventy-five by the time he left. He recognized for that ministry to achieve more health and growth, some major issues would have to be addressed. He understood that he was not clear on what all those issues were and that he didn't have the real leaders behind him if he had wanted to implement significant changes. He was delighted to become the pastor of this new congregation since it averaged 120 in worship each Sunday. The job paid more, he had an assistant in the office, and the leaders told him that they hoped to hire a youth pastor, at least on a part-time basis, by the end of Fred's first year of ministry.

As he sat behind his desk, his books around him, his diplomas on the wall, his favorite lighthouse prints strategically placed, and his favorite sports team posters displayed prominently, he was filled with conflicting emotions. On the one hand, he was delighted to be in this new ministry. He felt that things had gone well yesterday. His wife and children seemed happy in their new surroundings. He was excited about the prospect of leading a ministry that would be healthy, growing, and not only touching those who came to the campus each week, but also reaching out and changing the community in which the congregation existed.

On the other hand, Fred was now wise enough to know that these feelings went with being in a brand-new situation, and most of his good feelings would be short-lived. He also felt a great sense of dread. Other than getting to know the people and the community in which he and his family now lived, he had no real understanding of what he needed to do to lead a healthy, growing congregation. As a result, he had no plans or strategies in place, even in his imagination. This knowledge almost paralyzed him. He knew that within a few short weeks he would spend far more time staring at the wall, and then more out of frustration than intention, he would keep busy with more and more care ministry that wouldn't lead the congregation to effective ministry. He realized it was Monday; Sunday would be coming in six more days. Within a week or two his days would be filled with tasks that would serve individual believers but not produce overall changes leading to health and growth. He knew that busyness and faithfulness didn't necessarily translate into fruitful, fulfilling ministry. These thoughts threatened to ruin the excitement of being new and having the opportunity to be a different pastor than he was in his previous charge.

Fred wondered whether his lot was to be that of many pastors in congregations across the nation: doing work but seeing little meaningful change, growth, and effectiveness happen. He was convinced God had called him to serve in the church as a pastor, and he wanted to be effective for God. He was honest enough with himself to realize that, rightly or wrongly, his significance was tied to his ability to lead a congregation to be effective, not just maintain or grow marginally. Yet he was also honest enough to admit he didn't know what to do. He was not sure how he would handle it personally and spiritually if his lot was to be that of most pastors he knew.

LEADERSHIP: CREDIBILITY AND COMPETENCE

Many in the church of Jesus Christ, particularly in North America, are crying out for leadership. The leadership problem the church faces is no different from that in the rest of the culture. Everyone says we need more leaders. Bookstores are filled with whole sections on leadership and related topics such as management, administration, change strategies, and so on. One major difference between congregations and the businesses that these books target is that businesses exist to make a profit and pay employees whom they can hire and fire, while congregations are mostly volunteer organizations with donors. The lack of leadership in the church world is more obvious since people follow a leader only because they want to—not because they must.

In the for-profit world and in the nonprofit world where congregations exist, people are much more willing to follow someone who is perceived as credible. People are looking for leaders who know who they are and what needs to be done and have a good idea of how to implement their ideas. In any culture people follow not because they want to keep their jobs but because they want to.

Most pastors are not natural-born leaders. They lack either the gift or the talent of leadership. Pastors are like most people since the majority of the population lacks the gift or the talent for leadership. Pastors, however, whether they desire it or not, are in a position of leadership. Even the majority of pastors who admit that they are not leaders and don't want to be leaders recognize they are spiritual leaders to some group of individuals. (A shepherd is a leader who leads sheep.) To be a pastor means that to hold a leadership position is unavoidable.

All pastors, including those who don't have the gift or the talent of leadership, must at times practice leadership behavior. Yet in the majority of congregations pastors don't see themselves as leaders, the congregations don't see them as leaders, and often key leaders in the congregations don't want their pastors to lead.

When pastors lack credibility, they don't see themselves as leaders, and congregations don't want them to be leaders. In most cases this lack of credibility is not related to character. Rather it is related to the key ingredient in gaining credibility: competency. People follow those whom they believe to be highly credible, and competency is key to being perceived as credible. The relationship between followers and leaders is based on trust. I won't follow someone I don't trust unless I'm forced by conditions beyond my control, whether those conditions are perceived or actual. The more credible (read: competent) the leader, the more followers trust the leader, and they demonstrate this trust by their willingness to follow.

Too often congregations have watched pastors come and go, each having varying levels of competency, but overall congregations recognize that most of them didn't know how to be competent in leading a congregation in the twenty-first century. I find that many pastors are like Fred in our story, who wants to make a difference, wants to lead, and wants to see changes that would produce effective disciples and effective ministries within the congregation and to the community, but doesn't know what to do and how to go about accomplishing such results.

Often I hear rants from pastors: "I attend all the 'insider' seminars, read the right books, and go to all the good websites recommended by other lead pastors, and yet when I walk into my office on Monday morning, I've no idea what to do. Not only do I not know what to do, I'm not sure where to begin, I don't know what will make me more effective, and I'm not even sure how to schedule my week. I learn and read really good stuff and have no idea how to translate good ideas and concepts into my life, my personal wiring, and my particular ministry. Also ministry is so complex I don't know where to start. All the stories the experts share neither work in my context nor seem to fit my context."

Of all the professions, pastors are probably least trained to be competent for the tasks of leadership for which they are responsible. This is not their fault, since seminaries or Bible colleges are not doing it (and let me say, seminaries can't do it or be expected to do it). However, it is the pastors' problem.

Pastors need training. We have seen a miraculous transformation in the congregations of our region, now named Growing Healthy Churches (GHC). God enabled us to plant an average of ten new congregations a year for the past eight years, many of which are now more than two hundred in average worship attendance. Baptism of new disciples improved from less than eight hundred a year to more than four thousand a year. One major reason for these results is that we are constantly training pastors (of both new and established congregations) to be competent in their roles. Such competency produces credibility that enables our pastors to be leaders whom people willingly follow, even though nothing requires them to do so other than the motivation of the Holy Spirit.

PURPOSE

The purpose of this book is to help pastors become more competent at their tasks of leading congregations, day in and day out. I answer two questions. First, what must be done in the first 365 days of tenure to eventually lead the congregation through systemic transformation? Second, what should be done each day of the week to accomplish necessary tasks during the first year as the pastor, and in all the following years, in order to stimulate systemic transformation?

Often I ask pastors two questions. First, how would you like to be called or sent to a congregation new to you, and the very first Sunday after you preached, the lay leader of the congregation says to you, in front of the entire congregation, "Pastor, we are delighted you are here, and we have made a covenant for the first two years to do whatever you tell us, with no questions asked"? The laity commits to carry out your mandates and ideas with all of their strength, minds, and will. Every pastor wants to know where this church is, realizing it doesn't exist anywhere in God's creation. Second, if you experienced such a congregation, would you know what to do next? Most pastors respond to the second question by saying they wouldn't know what to do.

Pastors should know their goals for the first year of ministry (particularly in congregations on a plateau or in decline). Pastors should also know how to function day by day in order to see the Holy Spirit lead congregations to willingly follow their pastors' lead (shepherds lead) and implement the mission the Lord Jesus Christ gave to his church (a community of disciples), which is to make new disciples on a regular and consistent basis.

ASSUMPTIONS

I should disclose some assumptions about pastors, congregations, and the perspective from which I'm writing. In preparation for this book I interviewed a number of effective pastors to see what made their pastoral experience so different from the current norm in North

America. These pastors served in a variety of settings, including rural, suburban, and urban. Their congregations have been different sizes, but most of them were beyond the two hundred barrier in attendance, which the majority of congregations never break through. (Most of these pastors were leading congregations that were under the two hundred barrier when they started.) The congregations being led by these pastors reflected varying philosophies of ministries, and the pastors themselves were of different ages, ranging from thirties to sixties. Many of the assumptions are based on what I learned from the pastors I interviewed, ministries I observed through hundreds of congregational consultations, and my own experience as a pastor, a seminary professor, and a mentor to pastors.

Some of the assumptions present parameters for the kinds of congregational contexts I address in the book. I hope that many of the concepts I share will fit into most situations, but some tactics or strategies may not relate to every situation due to the idiosyncratic nature of ministry. Most of the time the issues being faced by pastors in local congregations are broad in nature, but when that is not the case, I make distinctions. However, I know from experience that I won't be able to think of all of the situations that pastors encounter.

Assumption One — Everyone Needs a Place to Be Bad

The successful stand-up comedian has perhaps the most challenging communication task for any speaker. The stand-up comedian is alone on stage attempting to be funny for people who have paid to be entertained. As a great comedian once said, every comedian needs some place to be bad in order to become good. The same principle is true for effective pastors. I had the good fortune of preaching in nursing homes all the way through high school, which was great since most of the people couldn't hear me. Every pastor I spoke with told me of failed ministry experiences before achieving some degree of pastoral success. Also, everyone said to me, "If I could go back even where God has blessed and do certain things differently, I would."

There are two good places to be bad. The first is a ministry position on the staff of a large, effective, growing congregation. This experience can be enhanced if the senior pastor and key staff members are willing to take on mentoring and coaching roles with you. If you can find such a position (as an intern or part-time staffer) while in seminary, extend your studies in order to be more involved in ministry than in academia. In such a position, you can learn the failures and successes of ministry where you will be mentored and protected. You also need to take the initiative to interact with the senior pastor and other effective staff members to learn why they have behaved in certain ways and how they have achieved effectiveness in their respective areas of ministry.

The second place to be bad is a solo pastorate of a really small congregation (usually one that can't afford a full-time pastor) while in seminary. In this setting you learn how to conduct ministry and behave when the congregation sees you as its pastor. You learn what often causes sheep to bite and act mean. You also begin to learn which hills you need to die on and which ones can wait for another time to be climbed. There is usually no pressure on you to promote growth and change. These congregations often exist as small places because they won't change. One of the best learning experiences is to try to lead change where nobody wants it.

Perhaps one of the worst places to be bad is a position, while in seminary, as an intern or part-time staff member in an unhealthy congregation that is not growing. You will likely observe a pastor who doesn't know what to do, does nothing, or does it incorrectly. Yet you don't have to live with those failures because you aren't the pastor. This common practice of sending an intern to a dying congregation is like sending a medical resident to watch a pathologist do autopsies.

Regrettably for many pastors, the first place they get to be bad is their first full-time role as a solo pastor. If this is your case, realize that it is a learning experience, and serve as well as you are able. Don't become discouraged. If you learn from your mistakes, you will be a far more effective pastor when you are called to lead your next congregation.

Assumption Two—Nobody Knows What to Do Initially

Seminary or Bible college doesn't prepare one to be an effective leader-pastor in this day and age. Most ministry training in seminaries assumes a somewhat Christian culture as the environment in which the pastor will serve, but pastors today (even in the Bible Belt) are called to lead congregations to minister effectively in a pagan culture.

In fact, seminary can't prepare an individual for the role of being an effective pastor. This statement is not an indictment of seminaries, unless they make the claim that they can prepare a person for such a position. All formal training for ministry, whether it is at the graduate or undergraduate level, is designed to prepare a person to think biblically and theologically. Academic training cannot by its very nature prepare someone to run a complex volunteer organization that requires business, political (managing the values and agendas of constituencies), social, psychological, and cultural skills. This is particularly true in a culture where many friends and critics alike see the church of Jesus Christ as irrelevant in general and to their needs in particular. They view leaders of congregations as out of touch with real life. No academic institution designed to train for any profession can do this. That is why medical students who have spent four years learning chemistry, biology, anatomy, and so on are then required to do more years of residency to learn how to use acquired knowledge safely with patients. Similarly, pilots first do ground training and then are required to conduct hours of flight training to implement all they have learned.

In talking to effective leaders who have become highly effective pastors, I found that they didn't know what to do when they started. Now it is true that these leader-pastors recognized themselves on a steep learning curve and had the skills to take the new knowledge they were gaining and implement it quickly, often with good results. But the fulfillment of the role took major learning and behavioral adjustments. This is even true for second-career leaders who may have been highly effective in their previous careers. After all, being an effective physician who is great at diagnosing complex diseases doesn't qualify that doctor to be a surgeon.

The illustrations about physicians and pilots point to two faulty assumptions that most Christians make about being a pastor. First, dealing with the threat of loss in the physical world requires more time and experience than does the threat of loss in the spiritual world. Second, pastoring effectively today is relatively easy, and anyone can do it. It is true that the gospel message is simple and one doesn't need a formal education to understand and believe it. It is also true that God calls the least of this world to confound the wise. However, it's also true that being called to serve God in a leadership role in the church of Jesus Christ requires a lot of hard work, diligence, wisdom, and mentoring from effective leaders. The process of helping people embrace God's healing for their whole beings should be taken with greater seriousness than training people to help others embrace God's healing for their bodies. The more pagan and complex the culture becomes, the more difficult the task of leading effective congregations.

All good pastors called to lead their first congregation start with the realization they just don't know how to fulfill the role. The first solution to all problems is defining the problem, and the problem for pastors is that they don't know how to implement the role they have been asked to fulfill.

Since the ministry of leading an effective congregation requires the ability to perform many complex behaviors, effective pastors move from professorial learning (in formal institutions) to behavioral learning. They practice by trial and error. They look for mentors who are effective at what they do and are just as effective in coaching others to do what they do. They function as apprentices and interns, even if they are the solo pastor of a congregation. Through a variety of means, they learn best practices from those who have practiced their craft well over an extended period of time.

The regret for many pastors and congregations is that pastors who have been pastors for a long time still don't know the job. In part this is the case because pastors thought they were prepared for the task on graduation from seminary or college. Another cause is that many pastors think they know the job, but the congregation won't allow them to fulfill their tasks or don't help them accomplish their tasks. Many pastors assume they are ineffective because congregations won't follow their lead and possess a low commitment in serving Jesus Christ. For such pastors the problem is not theirs since the fault rests with the congregation.

It's also true in too many cases that congregations don't want the pastors to perform the required tasks for health and growth since doing so would force many in the congregation out of their comfort zones. In many of these situations no one can lead the congregations to be effective. That's why pastors and denominations should avoid such congregations. When it is clear they won't follow our Lord's mission for the church, we should follow our Lord's advice and ignore them.

I find many Christians and many congregations do want competent pastors, and they are frustrated when they don't have them. They want competent pastors because they want to be part of a congregation that is fulfilling the mission that God has created the church to accomplish. It is crucial for all pastors to start with the assumptions that they haven't been adequately trained since adequate training is an impossibility, and they, like all pastors, don't know what to do, at least initially.

Assumption Three—Congregations Only Know It When They See It

The innovations that change paradigms generally don't come from what customers want. Customers clearly understand improvement since improving the quality and efficiency of goods or services meets felt needs. However, true innovation comes from the dreamers and experimenters who conceive things not thought possible by most people. Those of us raised in an analog world knew we needed electronic devices that would function faster and take up less space. That was our need. It took innovators, not their customers, to conceive a digital world that brought us into a whole realm of possibilities and options of which no customer ever dreamed. And while things moved faster and devices became smaller, they also produced applications only the dreamers could see.

The same concept is true for congregations. Most congregations know they want ministry to occur with more effectiveness, involving more people, with resources leveraged to accomplish miraculous ends. Yet most have no idea what it takes to move innovatively from dysfunction, plateau, stagnation, and even decline and death. First, they have seldom seen it occur. Second, very few have experienced such change firsthand. Third, if they did know what it entailed, it would scare them. When I conduct a congregational consultation, I never ask members why their local body is not growing, if that is the case, because they don't know. Even in growing congregations, few people, often including leaders, understand why. If most pastors don't know what to do, there are few, if any, laity who can tell them what their role should be. The laity will share with the pastor what they want the pastor to do for them or their group. But they usually don't know what an effective pastor does to lead a congregation to conduct its mission well.

Added to this individual and organizational ignorance is a rising hubris in congregations that often stymies systemic change. So many congregations have lost so much that they take pride in what is left in their situation and that pride hinders their ability to experience great transformation.

Because of our Baptist heritage, my organization, Growing Healthy Churches (GHC), functions in a call system, where congregations call their pastors. (I also interact with bishops, district superintendents, and others in an appointment system. The issue I want to address is obvious; it is just handled differently.) When congregations call pastors, I'm amazed at their arrogance in thinking they know how to search for, select, interview, and call new pastors. The majority of established congregations in our nation are on a plateau or declining, pastors are not equipped to fulfill their tasks, and congregations don't know what is involved in the job of a pastor-leader. And yet, search teams think they have the answers and don't need help. Also, no matter how small or dysfunctional a congregation is, it thinks the next Apostle Paul is just itching to be its pastor. Such congregations don't realize that the pastors they need (because they know what to do and have done it) are not even interested in leading their small group or their large dysfunctional congregation.

Hubris is also evident in small declining congregations that allow their pride to stop pastors from trying to do the right things. Buildings become monuments simply because they are old or historic. Places within buildings are hallowed and regarded as untouchable because of who gave objects or furniture. Many congregations treat their facilities better than the people who inhabit them or need to inhabit them. Or if buildings are not sacred, certain practices or people are made that way because of past victories. Congregations allow their pride in facilities, past practices, or key leaders (dead or alive) to stop meaningful change for the future.

Assumption Four—Call Doesn't Guarantee Competence

This assumption is based on the current experience of pastors and congregations, not a theological foundation. First, some of us debate whether there is such a thing as a "call" to the pastorate. I believe God directs people into roles within the church of Jesus Christ. I also believe God places gifted people in the body for the good of the church. However, I'm not sure whether a distinct call to the ministry exists (for example, pastor, missionary, and so on), either theologically or practically. Every Christian is called by God to be a follower of Jesus Christ, and in that sense all Christians are called. Also, I don't think the experiences of a Jeremiah or an Apostle Paul are the norm for most believers. Yet today as I interact with many pastors, regardless of their competency or lack thereof, I'm told that God called them. Assuming they are correct, it is clear as we look at the pastoral landscape that calling (whatever it may or may not be) doesn't guarantee competency.

We are told that each one of us is to develop the gifts that God has given us. Therefore, if someone in the role of pastor affirms he or she has the gift of pastoring—again, whatever that is—it is clear that person needs to develop that gift. By the way, many pastors I meet don't list "pastoring" as their key or prominent gift. Perhaps "pastor" has become a cultural position, not a role attached to the gift of pastoring. In any case if the majority of pastors claim the gift of pastor, it is again clear that such gifting doesn't relate to competency.

Just believing that one who is in the role of a pastor of a congregation either has the gift of pastor or is called to be a pastor, or both, doesn't guarantee that one will be competent in fulfilling the gift or exercising the call. It is possible to help pastors become far more effective at what they do. Without knowing what to do and doing the hard work of learning and implementing key principles and practices, calling and gifting don't guarantee someone's effectiveness. Hiding behind the concept of call to justify ineffectiveness is, I believe, spiritually and morally unjustifiable. If one states that God has called one, one has a stewardship responsibility to become as effective as possible in fulfilling all that goes with that call.

Assumption Five—There Is Hope

The first four assumptions listed here, though truthful, are negative and could be quite discouraging. Since no one knows what to do initially, pastors do need a place to be bad. Also, since congregations don't know what they need, we can understand why often an ungodly hubris arises. And if we are honest that however we view ourselves as pastors, whether called, gifted, or just placed in a role to lead a congregation, we need to learn how to handle well the place in which God has put us. But if we accept only these four assumptions, all I have done is create frustration, anger, and guilt.

There is hope because God wants to see the church grow and be effective, because some pastors are highly effective, and because my organization experiences almost every week pastors who were not effective but are now growing in their abilities to lead congregations to health, growth, and reproduction. God equips people who receive gifts. The problem is that most have looked in the wrong place for the resources that can equip them well.

I'm writing as a pastor who, for more than a decade of ministry, didn't know what to do and didn't know how to lead a congregation effectively. Eventually I learned from being on staff with another pastor who understood how congregations function well in our nation, understood the culture, and knew how to produce godly ministry in the human situations of church life in the then twentieth century. I learned from an effective leader. Some years later I had the opportunity to observe, up close and personal, a megachurch pastor lead. I watched and learned. Working with and learning from some of the most effective pastors in North America, Australia, and New Zealand have allowed me to learn the job and to know what to do. In essence God has been very gracious in teaching me what I didn't know and helping me become effective in serving God as a leader in the church of Jesus Christ.

A greater joy than my personal transformation has been the opportunity to train, mentor, coach, disciple, and help hundreds of other pastors and watch them learn and practice what I have been able to learn and practice. In our region of now 230 established and new congregations we call Growing Healthy Churches, we have seen and continue to see more and more pastors learn their roles and fulfill them with effectiveness. As I work in Canada, Australia, and New Zealand, the same thing is happening. Even more encouraging is seeing it happen across denominations (especially in mainline and evangelical ones), in all different sizes of congregations (from twenty-three to more than two thousand in worship), with both men and women, and in different racial and ethnic settings.

There are people who know what to do and are doing it. There are also many people who know what to do and want to help others make it happen in their experience.

A caveat: as I train others, some have the ability to take what they have learned and implement it well on their own without too much more assistance from me or others. Many learn and can change but need to be in a system where they are continually and intentionally coached or mentored in order to see the changes take effect and produce effective ministry results. My goal is not only to help pastors but also to work with denominational and associational church leaders to create such systems. Having effective systems in place across a group of congregations helps every pastor and congregation to be more effective.

I have been interacting and continue to interact with these effective pastors in order to continue to learn and to help other pastors learn. The essence of what I have learned as a pastor and what I'm learning from other effective pastors is the basis for this book.

I know there is hope. I have experienced it as a pastor. I have observed it with colleagues and friends who are pastors, and I have seen it happen with pastors I have trained. Competency is within reach for most pastors at varying degrees of effectiveness.

PARAMETERS: YOU MUST START SOMEWHERE

All accountants, lawyers, physicians, auto mechanics, elementary school teachers, and graphic artists need to know basic information about their work. Yet the way a local accountant serving "mom and pop" businesses functions is somewhat different from a national accounting firm serving major corporations. One book does not fit all in any area, including leading congregations effectively. There is one sense in which this book will help all pastors and key lay leaders in congregations. However, it needs a target in order to be of assistance to readers. I hope many pastors find the book helpful, including those who lead effectively and well. (For them it may be a resource to use in mentoring other pastors and interns who are a part of their ministry.) My target, though, is primarily pastors who really don't know how to lead their congregations with effectiveness, regardless of how long they may have been fulfilling the pastoral role. Also since congregations are in different places, I need to establish guidelines about the congregation and the pastor leading that congregation.

Parameter One: a single or multicharge congregation(s) employs the pastor (female or male) full-time. I'm not writing about those who are employed in other jobs while leading a congregation on a volunteer or part-time basis, although my description of what needs to be done will fit such people. What won't fit such people is how they use time to implement the things I discuss.

Parameter Two: the pastor is single or married and may or may not have children. I'm assuming there is no major (medical, psychological, and so on) issue in the pastor's immediate or extended family that will require extended time, attention, or care. I'm also assuming that the pastor's spouse, regardless of her or his situation, is supportive and in agreement that this person should be in the pastoral role. Later on, I will discuss how to handle marriage and family relationships.

Parameter Three: the pastor is in his or her first, second, third, or even fourth call or appointment and still doesn't have a clear picture of what it takes to lead an effective ministry that produces congregation health, growth, and reproduction.

Parameter Four: the congregation(s) for which the pastor is responsible is either on a plateau or not growing regardless of size. The primary size of congregations I have in mind as I write is between twenty and two hundred in average worship attendance.

Parameter Five: the congregations are located in cities, towns, suburbs, exurbs, and rural areas. Some inner-city or extremely rural areas are culturally more difficult to lead, although we have experienced success in some cases. Yet every place I go to consult with a pastor and congregation I'm told why it is difficult to impossible for a congregation to grow in that area. This excuse has been proved invalid on many occasions.

Parameter Six: these congregations don't possess an abundance of resources although in most cases they have more resources than they think if all the sacred cows are taken off the table and become negotiable. "Sacred cows" include buildings, property, foundations, schools or preschools, designations of money made by church leaders (not donors), and so on.

Parameter Seven: God wants and expects the church to grow by making more disciples for Jesus Christ and to serve people, as the hands and feet of Jesus Christ, in any community. (This assumes the "hands and feet of Jesus" are consistent with the heart and will of Jesus.)

THE TEMPLATE: GETTING FROM HERE TO THERE

The major reason that most pastors and congregations are ineffective is due to our current understanding of the church of Jesus Christ. In chapter 2 I articulate my understanding of the nature and purpose of the church and its implications for the twenty-first-century church in our nation and in nations like ours. In one sense chapter 2 presents my theological assumption on which everything else is based, including effectiveness. Congregations that are growing without understanding and believing this assumption may be practically effective but are biblically and theologically ineffective. Also in this chapter I develop the role of the leader or pastor. Each individual pastor's understanding of the nature and purpose of the church determines that role. Therefore, pastors need to be clear on what they believe and in what way those beliefs are to be implemented in ministry. Such understandings are crucial, and they become even more important when the pastor's understanding is 180 degrees different from that of the congregation he or she leads.

Chapter 3 answers the first question I raised in discussing the purpose, which is, what are the pastor's goals in the first 365 days of ministry? I answer this question in the context of a congregation that has been on a plateau or in decline in relation to attendance and financial growth for at least three years. I'm assuming that transformational pastors understand that systemic transformation is required in such contexts. Therefore, it is important for pastors to lead transformation from the very first day that they begin ministry with a particular congregation. Also, unless the proper groundwork is laid, transformation will not occur, and pastors' attempts to achieve transformation will lead to its rejection not only initially but also for a number of years following the attempts.

Chapters 4 through 10 suggest the pastor's responsibilities for each day of the week beginning with Monday and ending with Sunday. In other words, I answer the question I'm often asked by pastors: "When I walk into my office on Monday (Tuesday, Wednesday, and so on), what do I do?" I put together what a workweek looks like so that a pastor may be effective. I clearly understand that no pastor is wired exactly like another and what one pastor may find effective, another may not.

CONCLUSION

My goal is to help pastors and congregations alike know what the pastor is to do and why. I meet this goal by sharing what effective pastors do and how they work each day of the week to produce such effectiveness. I want pastors who have read this book to have a much clearer understanding of their role and how to live out that role week after week.

Having this information will be of far less help for many pastors unless those pastors can be placed into denominational and associational systems that provide continual coaching, mentoring, training, and accountability. God has provided all of God's servants with differing degrees of abilities. Many of us need the intentional help of others to fulfill the complex task of leading a congregation with greater effectiveness.

CHAPTER 2

IS MISSION POSSIBLE REALLY MISSION IMPOSSIBLE?

Megan put the finishing touches on next year's calendar of events. She was good at this, and she knew it. After all, this was her eighth year of professional ministry, leading her second congregation as the pastor. She knew that God had given her gifts and talents for administration and organization. She had used them in the corporate world before attending seminary. Her track record at seminary had been stellar, and her denomination leaders recognized her ability to serve with distinction in the life of the church.

Her first pastorate went well. Perhaps that was because the situation was so dire when she arrived to lead the congregation. The population of the small rural community had not changed much for several decades. However, that was not the case of the congregation. The two pastors who preceded her had been disasters. Neither man was very personable, and both seemed to possess few, if any, skills or talents for organization. The result was a congregation that might need to close if the exodus of people was not turned around. Megan knew that one good thing about following pastors who had done poorly was that the congregation had few expectations for her leadership.

Her sparkling personality, her skills in organization, and her sensitivity to people resulted in a congregation that moved from expecting death to having hope for life. As many of those who had left heard that the new pastor was not only personable but also disciplined, organized, and energetic, they returned to see whether what they had heard was true. After four years of Megan's leadership, the congregation returned to the attendance level it had been a decade ago. When she left to go to her next charge, the people grieved her loss deeply because they loved her so much.

She knew the new congregation was different. This congregation of around 150 in worship each week, which was almost double the size of the congregation she had just left, was filled with teachers, small-business people, and managers and leaders in the local plant. They expected their pastor to plan well and lead them through the ecclesiastical calendar each year. They were delighted with Megan. Advent and Lenten services were carried out with planning and excellent implementation, with each person knowing her or his responsibilities ahead of time. Megan's preaching and visitation schedules enabled her to remain in contact with most of the people, and the church leaders knew they had a pastor who understood her profession well and acted with integrity, care, and love for the congregation.

As Megan stared at her computer with the completed yearly calendar now done and ready to be printed for the church leaders, she thought again of the doubts that had been plaguing her for the past year. She had finally shared them with her spouse last week over dinner. They had talked long into the night about what she was feeling. The bottom line of her concerns was, is this all there is to ministry? She was fulfilled when people were helped, when those hurting were comforted, and when she with others would serve every month in the local food pantry. All of those things, while good, provided her individual satisfaction about her ministry. Yet there was little fulfillment from leading a group of people to somehow change the world of their community.

She was honest enough to admit that in her last church almost all the growth had been the return of people who had left because they were dissatisfied with the two previous pastors. The congregation had not grown with new people, and the community still had about the same number of people involved in religious life as when she first arrived. Her current congregation, while delighted in her ministry, was not growing in any significant way. She often felt that all she was doing was keeping the machinery of church life well greased and oiled for those who had been Christians for a long time.

In her previous, corporate life, such results would have gotten her fired. Yet her bosses were impressed with her administrative and organizational skills, and her personality was such that almost everyone liked her. In corporate life, she was expected to produce and create a profit for the company. This meant change and growth in order to be effective. Efficiency was good, but effectiveness was demanded. She knew that congregations don't exist to make profits, but she also knew that Jesus had not called her to maintain the status quo, no matter how well she did it. Although she knew what to do in the corporate world, she didn't know what to do in the church world.

Megan knew that planning liturgies, organizing Christmas events, aligning volunteers for food banks, serving in denominational roles, ministering well to those in need, and so on were good and necessary things to do. However, if that was all there was and all her work and effort produced no change in lives corporately and individually, she was not sure how long she would last.

THE FUNDAMENTAL QUESTION

The most fundamental question facing the church of Jesus Christ in our nation today is *what is God's purpose in creating the church*?

Our theological understanding of its purpose and nature determines what we expect the church to be and how we expect people leading the church to act. The church of Jesus Christ in North America, along with Europe, Australia, and New Zealand, is not seeing the growth and expansion that are almost the norm in many other nations. While some congregations in our nation are doing well and some areas of denominational life are seeing transformation and reproduction, that is not the overall picture. Nationally the church of Jesus Christ appears to be losing in its ability to positively impact the culture and see statistically significant, regenerative growth. I believe this phenomenon is a result of a belief about the very nature and purpose of the church of Jesus Christ.

What we believe shapes our values, and our values shape our behaviors. In the church of Jesus Christ in our nation, our belief about the church shapes the behavior of the church's leaders as well as Christians who are the church, the body of Christ. If leadership is crucial, the beliefs of the leaders must change if there is to be any hope of seeing changed beliefs in the body (the church). If the beliefs don't change, the behaviors won't change.

Two questions illustrate this fundamental topic:

- Was the church established to be the custodian of the saints?

- Was the church established to carry out God's mission of redemption?

When I ask these questions, I ask them in a primary sense. A church on a mission does need to care for the saints who are carrying out that mission. A church that is the custodian of the saints does believe in and can employ strategies for mission and seeing the work of redemption accomplished. However, is the church fundamentally designed to be a place for saints to worship, grow, develop, and be prepared to carry out God's mission, or is the church by its very nature a missional entity that does worship, discipleship, and other activities in missional ways, designed more for what it achieves as an entity in the accomplishment of the mission, both corporately and individually?

34

In my first three books I use military metaphors, which some readers have found difficult in light of the events of the last two decades. I use such metaphors for several reasons. First, our Lord and the Apostle Paul used such metaphors since they illustrate truth from both everyday life and the Old Testament. Second, I use them to communicate the gravity of dealing with spiritual life-and-death issues. Third, I believe the pacification of the church has diminished the need to wrestle with spiritual warfare between our Lord and the evil one. I also recognize that as a child of World War II, I was highly influenced by that war and its aftermath. Therefore, I try to avoid such metaphors in this book. Having said that, I hope readers will allow me one that clarifies the difference between seeing the church in terms of carrying out mission and seeing it in terms of serving believers.

During World War II, a battleship was viewed as a missional entity. It was designed to bring together a group of people who individually and corporately would engage in the mission of winning battles and ultimately a conflict. The people were fed, provided places for rest, and trained when not engaged in a particular battle. All of these things were done in relation to a mission. A separate ship may have served as an R & R (rest and recuperation) ship, taking soldiers who had been fighting a battle and who needed time to rest, relax, and play. When the soldiers were on the R & R ship, the mission was to serve them and their needs, not win a battle. However, when rested, the soldiers would go back to their respective battles, individually or corporately. This is the difference between the two questions. For many people, the church is designed for the betterment of Christians, not as a tool for the corporate mission of redemption. For others, the church is a place that mobilizes believers for the mission and helps them accomplish it corporately as the church.

Our view of the church affects the role of the leader, in this case the pastor. Again, consider the battleship. The captain of the battleship sees everything in terms of achieving the mission of winning the next engagement. Eating, sleeping, training, and designating rest times are all done in ways to make sure the mission is not hindered.

The captain of the R & R ship makes sure that the individual needs of the people on the ship are met. She or he is not intent on mobilizing the group to achieve a mission; instead, the focus is on helping each individual get rest, food, and fellowship, so when those on the ship are called to engage the enemy on their own or with their group, they will be ready. The roles of the two captains are very different since the purpose for which the ships were created and commissioned is very different. In the story at the beginning of this chapter Megan was a great captain of an R & R ship. Yet she was frustrated with being given behind-the-lines responsibilities rather than being a leader who mobilized people for missional accomplishment.

A REST AND RECUPERATION CHURCH

I believe the church of Jesus Christ is doing so poorly in North America because the church is most often seen as a custodian of the saints. Most Christians believe in mission, but I sense that most Christians don't view the church as a missional entity designed more to mobilize believers than to serve them. I will develop an apology for the church's being missional later in this chapter since I believe that is what the Bible teaches. If the apology is correct, then the downfall in our nation is that we are not leading the church in general, and individual congregations specifically, to be and do what the Lord of the church intended. The fallout from an incorrect belief is to be expected if we are not doing what our Lord desires. At this point, I want to articulate what I perceive as reasons for the church's being led more to please the saints than to accomplish the mission that Jesus Christ intended.

Growing up in the 1950s, I often heard pastors, Sunday school teachers, my parents, and others state that living in the United States meant living in a Christian culture. Looking back over the twentieth century causes me to wonder what they meant since much that happened in that century and the previous ones was far from being Christian. Racism, the treatment of the poor, and the role of women in the culture, just to name a few examples, reflected significant national sins demonstrating that our culture was far from being Christian. We didn't live in a Christian culture.

We did live in a culture where the practices and beliefs of Christians were at least stated as the practices and beliefs of the culture. People regarded themselves as Christian in name since they at least verbally practiced the Golden Rule, had Bible reading and prayer in schools, labeled social misbehavior as sin, and promoted truth, honesty, and integrity as virtues that all should follow. The problem faced by the church was helping people understand that living well in the culture, while good, didn't make them regenerative before God. True Christianity begins with recognition of sin and the need to embrace the atoning work of Jesus Christ. All practical goodness in how we live comes from honoring the God who has graciously provided eternal life in Jesus Christ. However, the basic tenets of the way that Christians should live were at least verbally validated by the culture in which the Christians lived.

This parallelism between the church and the culture has today disappeared. Christian beliefs apart from regeneration produce in the lives of unregenerate people a lifestyle of form without substance. Cultural values that appear to be Christian are used to promote evildoing. The sins reflected in the twentieth century along with world wars and a world depression led to what we might call today in the United States a pagan culture. The problem is, the world in which the church existed changed, but the church in the United States mostly still acts as if it is living in the twentieth or even the nineteenth century.

As a result, Christians still consider the church's primary purpose as providing those things that will help them be better Christians. Often mission in evangelical circles is denied because Christians want to go deeper in their study of the Bible. In charismatic circles mission is often denied because Christians want more corporate experiences for feeling, knowing, and being in the presence of the Holy Spirit. In mainline congregations the focus is often on maintaining the traditions and the liturgical calendar, even if the behaviors reflected in such practices are meaningless, even for the few who participate, while minimizing any possibility of doing mission.

A second reason for denying that the church is to be missional is the influence of consumerism on Christians individually and congregations collectively. Almost everyone attends a local congregation as a consumer. The basic question being asked is, "If I attend here, what will you do for me?" The problem is exacerbated in that the longer people have been Christians, the more often they act as consumers, since they know what they want and often know how to get what they want. Even some individual congregational and denominational missional endeavors enable consumer Christians to feel better about themselves, in that they are giving back usually to people they perceive to be beneath them, and to allay some of the guilt produced by living a consumer and, in comparison to most of the world, a wealthy lifestyle.

The result of these forces working together is creating within our nation a church that overall is in decline and one that is seeing fewer and fewer people become brand-new disciples of Jesus Christ each passing year.

A MISSIONAL CHURCH

A missional church assumes that God is a missionary God who has been working since the fall of the human race to bring women and men back to a place of reconciliation with God and with God's purpose. This assumption is behind God's purpose in creating the nation of Israel in the Old Testament and the church of Jesus Christ in the New Testament. These two entities, while providing great benefit to those who were and are part of each, were designed primarily to carry out the missional nature of God's heart.

Early on in the Scriptures God tells Abram that he is being selected and blessed so that all the peoples of the earth will be blessed through him. In giving his nation the Law, God reminds them that the whole earth is God's, but the Law sets the nation apart to function as a kingdom of priests to all the other nations (Gen. 12:1-3; Exod. 19:4-6). God used the nation of Israel to provide light and blessing to the nations. In fact the prophets speak of the role of Israel to be a light to the Gentiles. That was why when the nation or its leaders sinned, God often judged not just because sin offends God's nature and person, but because of what the sin did to hurt God's reputation with the nations.

The nation of Israel, from God's perspective, never functioned in a vacuum. God created the nation to serve God's missional purposes for the world. The problem for the nation was that Israel assumed that all God did was primarily for its benefit and was more concerned with its agenda and needs than with what God wanted to accomplish in the mission of reconciling the world to God. In many ways the church of Jesus Christ in our nation acts like Israel.

In the four Gospels our Lord is very clear about his mission. He tells us that he came to do the will of the Father, which is to provide redemption for the world. Elsewhere he states that he came to seek and to save those who were lost. It is in this context of mission that Jesus speaks of establishing his church. After making that statement, he gives us the purpose for which the church will be created: to keep the evil one from prevailing in his mission. Like the nation of Israel, the church was designed to promote and achieve God's mission in the world, which is to bring sinful women and men back to God. Our Lord, in the passage often referred to as the Great Commission, reminds his followers that their mission is one of reproduction.

The book of Acts in its inception states that the work of the church is missional, with our Lord letting his followers know that they are to move out from Jerusalem to the uttermost part of the earth. Throughout the book, we see God intervening every time the church stops following its missional mandate. In fact God allows the church to face persecution in order to get the believers to move out from Jerusalem and achieve the mission that they have been called to pursue.

Although preachers often state that God allowed persecution in order to scatter the church, they seldom follow up with a significant implication. That is, God thought the mission of the church so crucial that God was willing to let some believers be physically sacrificed so that the rest would do what Jesus commanded. Today we in our nation are not facing physical death, but the God of the church is allowing congregation after congregation to die to help us see that the church must return to its missional mandate.

In their letters, the apostles constantly wrote of the need to share the faith they were developing and explaining to others. Paul spoke of being highly motivated to communicate the message of reconciliation. He also seemed not to care who preached the gospel or what their motives were, as long as the gospel was preached. After telling us how we in the church are a set-apart people and a nation of priests, Peter stated that such has happened so we can preach the praises of God, who has brought us from darkness to light. He then developed how we are to live submissive lives to various authorities primarily as an evangelistic tool.

Jesus reappeared to the Apostle John to provide his final revelation. The setting of this scene was to provide messages to specific congregations with which John was familiar. In dictating letters to the seven congregations Jesus was very clear that their candles would burn brightly if they did what he instructed. If they failed in their mission, their candles would be extinguished. The Lord of the church is extinguishing candles right and left in our nation today because we have moved away from seeing the church as missional.

Implications of Being Missional

Although strategies and tactics are crucial in carrying out a missional mind-set, missional congregations are not about strategies and tactics. Being missional involves an understanding that leads to a clear choice. Once congregations make that choice, strategies and tactics are crucial in implementing the choice. The understanding is that God didn't create the church for Christians (meaning that it exists primarily for their benefit in developing as disciples). God created the church to mobilize Christians to reach their world (to do that well, Christians need to develop and mature). It is a matter of purpose or mission. To use a business term, the church serves two customers: those who are already disciples and those whom the church is attempting to help become disciples. In light of this understanding, the choice is that the unbeliever is the primary customer and the believer is the secondary customer. Once the understanding is clear and the choice has been made, leaders are then ready to develop tactics and strategies.

We must not confuse what today is known as the *seeker* strategy with the term *missional*. Most seeker congregations with which I'm familiar see themselves as missional. Adopting the seeker strategy is one way a congregation can be missional. However, I'm aware of many congregations that are not seeker but are missional. I know of congregations that sing hymns, use an organ, and preach expository sermons that are quite missional.

A missional congregation understands that its bottom-line purpose is to achieve the mission of continually making more and more new disciples for Jesus Christ and then equipping those disciples to develop and be committed to a ministry of reproduction, both individually and collectively. This purpose determines a most basic choice, which is to honor those people who are spiritually separated from God and all the needs arising from that status over those people who are already disciples of Jesus Christ. Yet disciples of Jesus Christ cannot be forgotten; they must be equipped to grow and develop so that they, too, might grow up "in Christ" in order to represent their Savior well in thought and deed, while reproducing by making more new disciples for Jesus Christ. Once that understanding is in place and the choice has been made, the congregation develops a strategy to implement the understanding and the choice.

Looking at the microcultural environment in which the congregation exists and determining how to best attract, reach, and make brand-new disciples in such an environment do this. In other words, the congregation is designed to fish for men and women in order to help them become followers of Jesus Christ. People who fish well understand that they must find the right bait, go where the fish will be attracted to the selected bait, and fish in a way that many fish are caught. In a congregation this means aligning all that the congregation does to catch fish. Everything—from who leads the congregation to which ministries are employed, to how those ministries are employed to the facilities used for meeting—works toward achieving the mission. These things are not done to please congregational leaders, meet the expectations of the Christians in the congregation, or meet culture norms that Christians expect in their part of the world. Missional congregations always start with the word of God and its teachings and then move to the "fish" being caught to design the style and philosophy of ministry the congregations will pursue. The more the design reflects the teachings of Scripture, the understanding of the fish, and the consistency of alignment, the better the mission will be achieved.

This is often why new congregations, or church plants, are more evangelistic than established congregations. First, new congregations need people. Second, new congregations are probably not going to attract Christians from established congregations, which mostly is a good thing. New congregations need to think of "doing church" in relation to the fish that are in their community. One doesn't fish for rainbow trout in the Rockies in the same way one fishes for salmon on the Columbia River. There is also greater flexibility in aligning the ministries of the congregation for effective fishing, whereas established congregations often have an entrenched culture that dictates the preferred behaviors for the fish already in the boat. Those fish usually don't want to change cultural preferences to catch more fish, even if such preferences have become ineffective for fishing. In some cases the large fish want to consume smaller fish for their own benefit.

Leading Missional Congregations

Missions are led, not managed or orchestrated by committees. This is often news to many congregations where denominational polities (structural organization) are based far more on the representative government models of either Great Britain or the United States than the Scriptures. Yet even these nations have recognized that in times of extreme crisis, strong leadership is required. If the experts are correct and the church of Jesus Christ is dying in the United States, Canada, Australia, and New Zealand, and if I'm correct in asserting that the church of Jesus Christ mostly is not acting as our Lord expected it to act, it is a crisis time that demands leadership. In GHC we have found that established dying congregations are not transformed without strong leadership. We have also found that starting new congregations that are healthy, growing, and effective demands strong leadership. Let me hasten to add that strong leadership is not dictatorship. Rather it is the marriage of responsibility with authority while demanding rigorous accountability of the leader. However, leadership is demanded to pursue a mission in a nation that sees the church of Jesus Christ as irrelevant and is populated by consumer Christians demanding that our Lord's church be run to meet their needs first.

Pastors and congregations can no longer engage in organizational schizophrenia. On the one hand, pastors and congregations alike have stated for years that the pastor's job is to be the spiritual leader of the congregation. Meanwhile the role of the congregation and its designated leader is to run the affairs of the congregation. Usually this concept means that the pastor preaches sermons on the weekend while helping individual sheep with their needs and problems throughout the week. On the other hand, the collective will of the sheep, through the decisions made by elders, deacons, or congregation, is not the pastor's purview. The congregation decides who participates in worship services, along with the style and substance of much that occurs in worship; oversees much of the educational ministry of the congregation; and definitely guards money and property. This distinction between leadership and chaplaincy is so unbiblical that we would laugh at it if it were not so much a part of most congregational cultures.

Let me provide just one illustration of the unbiblical nature of this concept. Most congregations I work with want the pastor to preach more about money. The reason is that every year the available financial resources in most congregations are dwindling. The expectation is that the pastor will tell the congregation that God expects and wants disciples of Jesus Christ to give. In other words the leaders expect the pastor to act as a spiritual leader, calling believers to the godly responsibility to contribute their financial resources. Yet when it comes to allocating, spending, and saving financial resources, the pastor usually has little say over how it is done. If giving is a spiritual act, distributing God's money is an equally spiritual act, which should be led by the pastor.

Congregational leaders expect the pastor to challenge members who don't attend services, confront those living in open sin, and comfort those who are sick and hurting. But when it comes to financial disobedience (not giving proportionately), that is none of the pastor's business. In many congregations the pastor is not allowed to know who gives and how much individuals give. The tragedy is that many congregations act this way and many pastors put up with it. Yet this is doublespeak if the pastor is to be the spiritual leader of the congregation.

The Leader

Perhaps the most basic requirement to be a leader or to consistently exercise leadership behavior is the desire to lead. You want to make a difference and are convinced that no one else is going to step up, so you must take on the responsibility. In many Christian circles this attitude is considered unspiritual. We are told that the first will be last and that the last will be first. We are told that if we want to take on some role to lead others, we are proud. We are conditioned to think leadership must be thrust upon us and we need to be dragged reluctantly into the arena of leadership.

It is true that we are not to seek positions of prominence to satisfy our egos and need for significance. It is also true that God has thrust some people into positions of leadership, such as Moses. However, according to the Apostle Paul, God wills God's will in us. If we stand idly by, waiting to lead out of false modesty, someone will step into the void, whether or not he or she is qualified to lead. As a very capable leader, David was ready to fight Goliath even when Saul and his own brothers attacked his motive. He knew that someone needed to step into the vacuum.

The desire within Christian leaders to want to make a difference comes out of the passion that God puts within us. Such passion is usually fueled by righteous indignation about situations we face. Passion not only produces vision it also produces a desire to make a difference for God. This is one of the problems that pastors now face since "the pastorate" is often seen as a profession much more than a calling or a burden placed on us like God did with the Old Testament prophets. A passion fueled by truly righteous indignation does a number of things in the hearts of pastors. It causes us to want to make a difference for God, no matter the cost. It produces a vision that says the status quo is unacceptable and there is a preferable future. It provides the courage to risk and do what needs to be done, even at the expense of our reputation and paycheck. It causes us to minister in places where we would typically not like to live and work long hours because without an investment of time we know little good will happen. Passion comes because we are doing what we do for the cause of Jesus Christ, not our political or social agenda.

A pastor who doesn't want to be a leader or consistently exercise leadership behavior needs to know she or he will probably experience a ministry of mediocrity. Those in a profession waiting for good things to happen will usually be disappointed.

In the first chapter I discussed that people follow leaders they find credible. I also said that a big part of having credibility is being seen as competent. I want to touch on key areas of competency, realizing that no one can become competent in these areas all at once. However, I think if pastors don't become competent in them, eventually they won't be called on to lead vibrant ministries. (I will expand on some of these areas in the next chapter.)

First, in this day and age there is no reason not to know what it takes for a congregation to become healthy and grow. The material is out there in books, articles, seminars, and blogs. The problem is wading through all the information, learning what is fundamental and what needs to build on the fundamentals. I'm still amazed at what pastors don't know about causes of decline or growth in a congregation. It is rare when I do a consultation with a healthy, growing church to find a pastor who knows little about producing congregational health and growth. If leading congregations is my business, in the right sense of the term, few know the business they are in. (I won't discuss this area of competency in the next chapter since there is so much material readily available to pastors, including my first three books: *Hit the Bullseye, Direct Hit, and Assaulting the Gates*.)

Second, pastors need to become competent in gathering people. Most pastors are waiting for people to come to them and to their congregation. Effective pastors know what needs to be done to gather people.

Third, pastors need to become much more competent in understanding the nature of money, how to get more of it, how to spend it wisely, and how money determines the effectiveness of ministry. I know most seminaries never discuss this. Yet failing to understand money will mean failing to get a grasp on effective ministry.

Fourth, pastors need to become competent in understanding the nature of congregational governance and how to have influence over the polity in which they find themselves.

Fifth, pastors need to become competent in how to relate to people in their congregations. In this area EQ is far more important than IQ.

Sixth, pastors need to become competent in learning how to read, understand, and adapt to their local culture. Effective pastors are really missionaries. They must become amateur sociologists who can help congregations remove cultural barriers and build cultural bridges.

Seventh, pastors need to know how to fish for the souls of women and men in the twenty-first century in ways that fit their local culture. Too often they still use cultural methods of evangelism that were great for the nineteenth and twentieth centuries but no longer work in the twenty-first century.

Leaders not only want to lead and work on becoming competent so people will see them as credible; leaders also want to help people see into the future. People follow those who enable them to believe that together the group can accomplish more and greater things than is possible for an individual. We live in a world where people are desperately looking for hope. Leaders provide such hope by offering a vision of a better and greater tomorrow. After all the word of God is correct when it states that without a vision, particularly a God-inspired vision, people live in chaos and often see their present existence as meaningless.

When leaders go into an undesirable situation, they recognize that their responsibility is to create a sense of urgency so that individuals and the group become dissatisfied with the status quo. The leaders then paint a picture of a preferable future that motivates people to reject the status quo in order to pursue a new and better tomorrow.

A missional God is looking for women and men who want to take on the responsibility of leading congregations to accept the mission that Jesus gave them. This is not an easy task, as the experience of many congregations and pastors bear witness. That is why leadership is needed. God is looking for individuals who possess a passion to make a difference. These leaders know that people will follow more willingly when they perceive that the leaders are credible. That is why competency is crucial. And leaders understand that followers expect leaders to have some insight into where God wants the congregation to go. Peaks need to be climbed, and once one peak has been ascended, there are higher and bigger ones to tackle. The joy of life is, by faith, taking on the challenges the Lord of the church places in front of his people.

CONCLUSION

Our Lord has not called us to an impossible mission. He has called us to a demanding mission that requires a cost from people willing to take on that mission either as leaders or as followers. Yet often today, as we look at the church scene in our nation, it seems as though mission possible has become mission impossible. I suggest the reason is that we have lost sight of the fact that Jesus has called us individually and collectively to mission. We have set our sights on taking what the Lord of the church created for mission and making it the custodian of the saints. This loss of purpose is the biggest theological and pragmatic problem facing the church and individual congregations today.

If we accept the biblical and theological concept that the church was designed for mission and that we don't get to relax until we are with our Lord in heaven, the impossible mission can become possible. Embracing the concept of mission means designing our congregations to achieve the mission by starting with those who are not a part of the congregation now, but will be as the Holy Spirit works through missional congregations. It also means understanding that missions are led, not managed, and the leader is called to inspire a group of sheep to change the community in which the sheep exist.

In Growing Healthy Churches, our kingdom network of congregations, God consistently proves through the transformation of dying congregations and the establishment of brand-new church plants that the mission is possible. Our pastors and planters are far from perfect, as are our congregations. However, we are consistent in demonstrating that our congregations are led by missional leaders, who are helping the members of the congregations understand that collectively we are on a holy mission from God and with our Savior's help we plan to win.*

* I encourage you to read Appendix One at this point. The few pages written by JD Pearring will provide wise insight into how pastoral leaders and church planters can work effectively in their initial dealings with a congregation.

CHAPTER 3

365 DAYS AND COUNTING

Pastor Charles sat at his desk, 364 days to go. Yesterday was his first official day at his new charge. A sense of excitement permeated the building as many in the congregation came to worship looking forward to meeting their new pastor. Realizing that such an atmosphere wouldn't be repeated until the congregation greeted their next new pastor, Charles thought the day went well. He prayed during his devotional time that such a day would be a long way off since he intended to stay many years.

Having finished his prayer time with God, he reflected on the events that had brought him to this day. He was as excited this Monday morning as his congregation was yesterday. He remembered how God had used circumstances to lead him from the business world into a life of pastoral ministry. It was not something he had planned in attending the university, but God had orchestrated his journey quite differently from what he anticipated. And now, for the first time, he felt ready to tackle this new assignment with confidence.

While in seminary he was the pastor of a small, struggling congregation, and he remained in that position two years after graduation. His attempts at leadership failed. The congregation did not grow, and he made so many mistakes he knew the people were relieved when he left. In some cases he tried to move too fast; in other instances he did not move fast enough. He backed away from key decisions he should have made and made choices that should have been postponed to a later time. On leaving that congregation, Charles and his family decided he would take two months off, at great financial cost, so that he could take time to pray and evaluate. He didn't want to repeat his mistakes. During this time, Charles began an aggressive leadership learning regimen on his own. He read in the areas of leadership, congregational health, and leading change.

His work paid off, and his next pastorate went much better. The congregation grew in average worship attendance from fifty-two to ninety-three in just three years, which led his denomination to recommend this new charge to him. He was convinced that not only had God led him to take this new position but also had been preparing him in his previous two pastorates to lead this congregation to serve their Lord well in the fulfillment of the mission of making new disciples. In one way this new congregation, which averaged eighty-five, could be seen as a step backward or at least a lateral move in terms of his profession. However, Charles was convinced that God had great things in store for this part of the body in this particular location. Charles knew he was primed and ready to move. Day two had already begun, and he couldn't wait to see how the next 363 would turn out.

Charles clearly understood that his job was to do his best and that it was God's responsibility to grow the church. Like the Apostle Paul, Charles wanted to be a wise master builder. He understood how to be faithful and committed. But Charles wanted to make sure he functioned wisely in his role of leading Christ's church. This congregation had been on a plateau for several years. It thought small; most of the congregations in the denomination and in the local area were of the same size or smaller. Yet the congregation also felt good about being solvent and debt free. They were proud of their facilities. Charles knew that what he would do this first year would determine God's destiny for this congregation and his tenure as the pastor. The way in which Charles functioned in the first year would require hard work, wisdom, and the spirit of God to produce full results.

He knew the clock was ticking and there was much to do. He also realized that only he and his spouse understood this, and he was grateful for her support. As far as the rest of the congregation was concerned, the new pastor was in place, and it was back to business as usual. But for Charles, his actions in the next 364 days would determine whether time would be redeemed or lost.

THE FIRST YEAR

Whether one is starting a new congregation or leading a congregation that is on a plateau or in decline, the first year is absolutely crucial. In the case of a new congregation, the leader is establishing characteristics, or DNA, that will be with the congregation until it dies. In an established congregation, the leader is beginning to change negative portions of the current DNA, while adding new elements to the DNA that will lead to transformation. The longer one waits to act decisively and positively, the more corrupted the DNA becomes; in some cases this makes it impossible for the leader to lead well over a sustained period. At this point acting decisively and positively doesn't always mean the leader is acting publicly. The leader may be very decisive in doing things behind the scenes that only become apparent later.

The first year also establishes the leader's credibility. People are looking for leadership and expect the leader to lead. Everyone is waiting to see whether the pastor will lead, how the pastor will lead, and whether the pastor possesses the wisdom and courage to lead well. Many pastors believe that when they arrive in a new setting, they must learn all they can about the congregation and the community, which is true. (Obviously the more pastors can learn before arriving, the more time they will have to implement a course of action.) However, while such learning is occurring, pastors still need to actively initiate a plan of action and take advantage of the opportunity that most people in the congregation will give them to be a leader and actually lead.

I conducted a series of interviews with pastors who went on to lead systemic transformation in their congregations. I asked them what strategies and tactics they implemented in their first year of ministry in order to help the congregation make key decisions that would lead to systemic transformation. Consider a number of these key decisions.

Few pastors have the gifts, talents, and opportunity to lead systemic transformation in their first year of ministry. Yet key decisions that are implemented during the first year often determine whether systemic transformation will be possible sometime in the second to fifth year of the pastor's tenure. Also, key decisions made early on will have ramifications for years to come.

There is no way one pastor can do all of the things described in this chapter. You need to select three, four, or five things to do, driven by the ministry context in which you find yourself. A clear understanding of what must be accomplished the first year in that particular ministry context is crucial. The pastors I interviewed did different things, but all of them had a plan or a set of goals they wanted to achieve. Even pastors who approached ministry more intuitively responded, when pressed, that certain things had be done if the congregation was going to be effective in fulfilling Christ's mission for the church.

Learn the Congregation

Whether pastors are in a call system or an appointment one, most know one to three months in advance which congregations they will be leading. A wise pastor begins to prepare for the new position while closing out the current ministry.

First, the pastor learns as much as possible about the congregation. The pastor should read the history of the congregation and, if possible, interview people who have been a part of the congregation for long periods of time. Look for times of congregational growth or decline. Contact former pastors and discuss their experiences; be sure to ask how and why they left. If possible, contact other pastors in the community, regardless of denomination, and discover their perceptions about the congregation. And if the leaders allow it, read the minutes from board and congregational meetings for the last two or three years. Read annual reports. Conduct interviews with key leaders, even if done by phone or e-mail.

Wise pastors who conduct research on the congregation before arriving are doing two things. First, they are learning the facts, good and bad. They need to be up to speed on key past events as well as current ones. Pastors gain credibility when members of the congregation realize their pastors know things that other pastors took two or three years to find out. Second, these pastors are reading between the lines. They are looking for the DNA of the congregation and determining which elements are good and therefore need to be retained and used as building blocks for key initiatives. They are also determining which elements of the DNA are negative and will at some time need to be addressed if the congregation is to move forward. For example, some congregations, with great regularity, reach a certain size in attendance and then split due to conflict. This is crucial information for pastors to have before arriving on the scene. They know ahead of time what one obstacle to growth is going to be, which is people stopping growth because growth threatens their personal status in the congregation. On the other hand, a congregation started years ago in order to make new disciples in the community has a DNA element that can be tapped to bring the congregation back to its original purpose.

Learn the Community

Second, the pastor learns as much as possible about the community. Go to the Web to gather demographic details. Study the most recent census data available from the US government. Check websites related to the Chamber of Commerce or other organizations involved in doing business or providing services in the community. Explore books written about the history of the area. The more the pastor understands the county, town, suburb, or city in which the congregation is located, the better. For example, people still go to San Francisco to make their fortune, just as they did in gold rush days. After becoming established in their professions, getting married, and having children, they often move to the suburbs to raise their families in a different environment than the city. These lifestyle choices impact the way congregations conduct ministry in that particular city.

Visits are in order if the pastor lives near the new community to which he or she will be moving. Learn how to navigate the community, find out about housing, schools, shopping, and so on, and observe people in public places. Learn from residents what they like or don't like about the community.

Develop a First-Year Plan

Third, the pastor needs to develop a first-year plan, that is, identify three to five major accomplishments, God willing, for the first year of leadership. While the pastor will be working on these things, the pastor should have some idea of the chronology in which the ideas need to be implemented and the key strategies and tactics required to see these goals achieved. This plan doesn't have to be elaborate, but it should be specific and clear. It is best to write it down, particularly if this is the first time the pastor has attempted to function in this manner.

One element of the plan should be naming the early victories to be achieved in order to build momentum. Most congregations in decline or on a plateau lack momentum. They are used to doing the same things again and again, thereby observing the monotonous behaviors that produce the same results. Such a course of action ruins morale and eventually communicates a lack of hope. Leaders understand that in such situations people need to see new things happening. Seeing new life, people become excited and have renewed hope.

Often achieving early victories does not lead directly to systemic change. If they do, that is really a double win. However, early victories demonstrate positive movement.

One area in which many pastors find early victories is helping the congregation increase curb appeal of the facilities. I interviewed one pastor who had led several congregational transformations. He explained that the first time he ever visited the campus of a new congregation that he was fairly sure he would be called to pastor, he walked all the facilities and grounds. On a self-guided tour, he wrote down everything that needed fixing, painting, rebuilding, and so on. He placed the list in a file, ready to be worked on once he was the pastor. He said that the first visit is the only time a pastor has fresh eyes to see the grounds and buildings. Once you become a part of the place, you never see everything the same way. This list also provided easy fixes during the first year he was the pastor and produced early victories. I will talk more about this later.

The last thing the pastor does before arriving on the scene should be the first thing the pastor does when she or he realizes that the congregation is interested in his or her leadership. A wise pastor knows that the moment a congregation becomes interested in having that pastor as its new leader, the pastor possesses the most influence for change. This is the time to negotiate. This is the time to seek concessions that will lead to change. This is the time to determine the areas over which the pastor will have clear jurisdiction. This is also the time to set deadlines for certain changes.

Even in appointment systems, the pastor and denominational representative can work on these issues together if they see themselves as a team, helping to bring change. A wise pastor negotiates before making a commitment to a congregation. Such negotiations also help a pastor see what leaders are open to considering and what they regard as untouchable. Such understanding helps the pastor determine whether this situation will or won't be a good fit.

Gather People

In all the interviews pastors identified one common denominator during their first year: building congregational attendance. Everyone understood the responsibility for getting people new to the congregation to attend. As one pastor put it, "The congregation had no momentum, and I knew that the best way to create momentum was to see new people attending on a regular basis." Another pastor said the best early victory is for the congregation to see that people are coming to church because of the work and efforts of the new pastor. Each pastor produced this phenomenon of growth in a different way, but everyone developed a strategy to make it happen.

As I work with pastors of congregations in decline or on a plateau across the nation, I find that many don't gather people, don't know how to do it, and in some cases are not be able to do it. Many pastors believe that their responsibility is to wait for people to come to them. Pastors need to learn how to invite people, connect with new people, and create visitor flow in order to encourage their attendance.

One congregation was located in a small town. The pastor told me that he soon learned that the people in the community didn't like the church and disliked a number of individuals in the congregation. He realized that even if members of the congregation invited townspeople, many townspeople wouldn't attend because of their negative attitudes toward those members. The pastor added that he spent the first year building rapport with people in the community, so when he did invite them to church, many would respond positively to him and his invitation.

Another pastor in a smaller community understood the importance of being with people in the community wherever they gathered. They needed to see that this pastor was there, supporting them, and was willing to become involved in the community efforts they deemed worthy. Now after close to a decade in that community, he and his congregation have made significant inroads in the public school system, the town government, and other community-wide efforts designed to serve the townspeople. This pastor has been invited to pray and offer guidance on many communal events because he is considered an integral part of community life.

Pastors told me that for the first few years in the congregation, they were the entire connectional system. Meeting people, greeting them, following up with them, and shepherding them through their orientation into membership and service were part of their job description. One pastor met new people each Sunday and asked them if they would visit with him a few minutes after church. When the service was over, he said to them, "I'm assuming you are looking for a new church home, and that is why you are visiting." If that was the case, he said he guessed they were not coming back because the experience was not a good one, which was true, since there were so many problems in the congregation. The pastor apologized for their poor worship experience and asked them to come back and help him improve the overall ministry of the congregation. Then he laid out the changes he foresaw in the next few years. Many came back because he was honest about what was happening and because they wanted to join him in improving the environment and changing the overall ministry of the congregation.

Another pastor always invited new people to come back again so they could have lunch with him the following Sunday. The next Sunday, he introduced the new people to individuals or couples who were members of the congregation, and they in turn invited the new people to return the next Sunday for the service and also for lunch with them. The pastor did this each Sunday, up to five or six times. In this way new people connected with other new people as well as members of the congregation. There was a good chance they would attend the congregation regularly because they made new friends.

Pastors in established congregations have much to learn from effective church planters. When new pastors start new congregations, they understand that the number one job is to gather people. Planters recognize that if they cannot gather people, they cannot grow a congregation, and if the congregation doesn't grow, the new church never gets started. Or if it does start, it often dies an early death because no one is coming. Pastors in established congregations cannot wait for people to come to them; they must go to the people. Often the pastor is the only person in the congregation who assumes the responsibility of meeting people new to her or him and inviting them to visit the weekend service. If the pastor does not do it when the congregation is on a plateau or in decline, it probably won't occur.

Create Big Events

Many smaller congregations in smaller communities, as well as ones in bigger towns and cities, seldom have a large and consistent flow of visitors on the weekend. Big events that increase visitor flow are crucial, particularly for pastors who may feel uncomfortable inviting people in the community to come to church. Big events also provide visibility for congregations, change congregational reputations (particularly for those that have a reputation of being insulated from the community), and generate morale as the congregational community works together on major projects.

To do big events well from the beginning, pastors should be aware of several issues. First, distinguish between advertising events and bridge events. Advertising events are designed to get the name of the congregation out in the community, recognizing that advertising events, while valuable, generate first-time visitors. Bridge events are designed to help people walk across a bridge of faith, eventually become new disciples of Jesus, and regularly attend the congregation.

Second, while designing the event, develop follow-up plans for contacting guests. There is no sense in doing big events if there is no plan for follow-up with people new to the congregation. All across the country congregations are learning that attendance at a big event, particularly if it is not in a worship service, does *not* translate into increased congregational attendance. These events may provide some visibility for the congregation; however, the ultimate social networking is accomplished by face-to-face contact.

Conducting big events is like dating. If a first date goes well, both partners hope the second date occurs soon after the first. Doing a great first event and not inviting people to another event for three months is akin to a guy not calling a girl for three months after a first great date. Wise congregations know what the second, third, and maybe fourth dates are (the next events) and how people will be invited to them before the first date occurs. At the big event, people are invited to an upcoming seminar the congregation will present for four weeks to help families in the community address various issues. Then at the seminar, people are invited to two back-to-back worship services intentionally designed to meet specific needs related to the seminar, with activities designed to educate and motivate their children. The congregation in essence holds big events to enter into a dating relationship with new people.

The bottom line is that if big events (the term *big* is relative to the size of the congregation and the community) are done well, they help create a flow of first-time guests to the congregation. This group of new people becomes a pool of individuals with whom the pastor can network and invite to become a part of the congregation.

Improve Curb Appeal

Many pastors I interviewed said that one of the first things they did was to increase the curb appeal of the buildings and grounds. (Wise congregations often hire an image consultant for such tasks.) Almost all the pastors used the same term: *curb appeal*. They did this for several reasons. First, they realized that many potential first-time visitors wouldn't come simply because of the looks of the grounds and/or the building(s). Second, these pastors felt that if visitors did come, they would be discouraged from coming again because the facilities and grounds reflected neglect due to deferred maintenance and care. Third, they recognized one way to achieve an early victory was to focus on the physical campus and its appearance. Such care also reflected good stewardship of the physical assets.

The pastors went about the process of changing curb appeal in a variety of ways. Some discussed the issue as part of their call or appointment and obtained firm or even tentative agreements up front to work on changes. Others took time in board meetings to literally walk the grounds and facilities. They pointed out issues and described how visitors would perceive and respond to apparent problems. Others took pictures of potholes, peeling paint, missing shingles, and so on, and reviewed them with the board or the trustees at their meetings. Still others shared feedback they had received from people in the community or from visitors. In some cases the pastors solicited the feedback, and in other situations they reported what people told them. In a few cases the pastor encouraged leaders to visit other congregations that were making various changes and renovations to see what was being done and learn the results in terms of visitor attendance and congregational morale. (Several of our GHC congregations hired a consultant initially to provide an overall plan for the required changes needed to increase curb appeal.)

The motivation for change was always presented in relation to the vision being cast by the pastor. The pastors talked about reaching children, youth, younger families, empty nesters, and older adults. They demonstrated how the facilities, rather than helping the vision, were hurting it. They pointed out that if God was going to do a new work in the congregation, it often started with seeing something new and bright in the facilities. Numerous pastors who have led transformation have discovered that improving the facilities encouraged longtime members to invite new people. In some cases the longtime members were ashamed of their facilities, even though no one articulated that shame. In almost all cases many longtime members were so proud of the renovations, they invited people to church to see the facilities for themselves.

Congregations are like many families. We often don't immediately address areas in our homes that need painting or fixing. After a while these things become so common to our everyday experience, we no longer see them. They just become part of our daily environment, and we do not deal with them. In many congregations physical problems have not been addressed, usually due to either a lack of finances or a lack of leadership, and as a result, the congregation no longer sees them.

However, addressing the physical needs is a way to improve morale and provide a beginning sense of momentum. People see things happening and realize that the new pastor is helping the entire congregation feel better about themselves and present a better image to visitors and to the community.

Energize Worship

One reason many congregations are on a plateau or in decline is that the weekend worship service has become routine, dull, and boring. Routine provides comfort for those familiar with the routine while at the same time reflecting boredom and a lack of imagination to those unfamiliar with the routine. All of us know that when a routine is changed, if even for a brief time, it brings delight. People who dislike their jobs often do so because it has become routine, which is why they like meetings, breaks, or vacations that alter the routine, and in some cases they are more energized to go back to the routine because somehow the old routine has been infused with new life.

Almost every pastor I spoke with knew that somehow the worship routine had to be dealt with, even if the changes were miniscule. In some cases it was the way the service was led or the new people who were recruited to lead the service. In other cases the routine was not changed, but a piece was added, such as a children's sermon, greeting time, or beginning announcements. In other cases there was an agreement to conduct a special kind of service on a monthly or quarterly basis that provided freedom from the routine. In other situations the order or structure of the worship service was not changed, but the way the routine was conducted was changed on a regular basis. Responsive readings, prayers, offerings, observing the Lord's Table, and so on were conducted in a different manner, providing renewed interest for participants.

Wise pastors tried to negotiate freedom up front, before they were called or appointed, so that they had a right to make changes. One pastor, who possessed musical talent, stood up with the worship leader every Sunday and played his guitar when the congregation sang, even though the worship style remained traditional, including a choir and hymns. He told me that after a few months, everyone became used to it. He told the congregation from the beginning that their worship needed to become more contemporary, so he purchased a set of drums and had them on the platform every Sunday, even though no one played them. After six months, people started asking him when the drums were going to be used.

Perhaps the most flexibility any pastor is given, even in very rigid situations where routine is valued, is in how the pastor preaches. It is true in congregations where some kind of expository preaching is expected that the form of the sermon has become as absolute as the content of the sermon. However, in most cases, the pastor is given great latitude in how to communicate the word of God. I know one pastor who was gifted with good communication skills, and he realized that if he preached well, in his context, it would help draw people. (Today this is highly unusual, since even the best preaching, with some exceptions, helps the pastor keep people, not draw them.) This pastor spent fifteen to twenty hours a week working hard on both his exegesis and his communication skills. He often preached in first- or third-person narrative form and used visuals to convey truth. His preaching was so different that people started to come to hear it. By the way, pastors will know soon whether they have such preaching skills, regardless of how they personally perceive their ability to preach. If many new people are not coming to services after twelve to eighteen months, it is obvious they are not gifted to preach with excellence.

The other key aspect of the worship experience that pastors can change, often with less resistance, is what occurs in welcoming the congregation. Several pastors said they worked hard at helping people get from their cars in the parking lot into the service, knowing they would be treated as highly valued guests. They understood that on Sunday morning, they could not be in their studies; they needed to be at or near the front door greeting people, especially new ones to the congregation.

Also, these pastors realized that greeting new people, in a collective sense, from the platform is something they do every week. Regular attenders hear the greeting each week. Often people are welcomed in a way that reflects boredom and insincerity. Pastors realize that first-time guests are being greeted for the first time, and like actors on Broadway after four hundred performances know to be fresh for a new audience, they greet new people as though it is their first Sunday to do so.

Other pastors told me that they worked on changing the dynamics of the room to make a smaller congregation seem larger. If they had permission, they took out pews in the back to encourage people to sit farther forward and to make the room appear to be fuller. Others used a makeshift platform so they could be closer to the people when they preached or led worship. Others used lighting, paint, fabric, banners, and other accoutrements to change the look of the room and make it seem lighter or darker, intimate, or more alive.

Improving the facilities and grounds is a no-brainer. Pastors leading change also worked intentionally at changing the dynamics of the worship service in as many ways as they could that first year. A dull service is not helped much, if at all, by paint and carpet. Recently painted, renovated, or cleaned facilities will only make the pain more bearable if something is not done soon about worship service dynamics.

Communicate

Many pastors I interviewed used their communication opportunities to begin to lead change. A number of them developed sermon series that laid out for the congregation a theology of the kingdom of God, the church of Jesus Christ, and/or God's missional nature in using spiritual institutions to reach women and men apart from God. The common theme behind the messages, regardless of the content, was that the congregation for too long was not following God's intended purpose in how and why it met. They wanted to address in a positive way that God had created the church of Jesus Christ as a missional entity. Congregations exist primarily not to serve members but to serve God's intended mission of reaching a world separated from God and God's love because of sin, disobedience, and rebellion. Several pastors preached multiple series to lay out for the people their understanding of God's revelation for what the church is and how it should act. Of course in these preaching series they were also casting vision for the future of the congregation. These pastors worked at communicating vision again and again.

Pastors also preached about how the congregation might implement God's revelation into collective and individual actions. They discussed evangelizing, conducting random acts of kindness, reaching out in both word and deed to those in the community facing extreme physical needs, getting involved in the lives of individuals and in community efforts, and so on. The sermons were on both theology and action. One congregation's leaders gave the pastor permission to use each Sunday morning worship service as a congregational Alpha experience. This experiment proved to be quite successful.

Pastors made sure that somehow in every worship service, some aspect of the new that was needed would be communicated, such as the vision itself, key strategies for implementing the vision, or God's reason for a missional vision and mission.

The interviewed pastors commonly took advantage of a second communication experience: the monthly board or council meeting. Pastors led the meetings and used the beginning time for leadership development and training. They also created urgency (one example being the poor curb appeal created by the facilities and grounds) and cast vision. They used time with ministry groups or in staff meetings or committee meetings held to oversee Sunday school, worship services, or even the planning for big events. Usually the leadership and vision time in board or council meetings was kept to thirty to forty-five minutes. The pastors made sure that most meetings had this component since it was crucial for future change.

Often pastors supplemented their verbal communication in worship services and board or council meetings with graphs, charts, bulletin boards, banners, pictorial displays, and so on. Today, such illustrations would include digital media. All printed materials carried messages and reminders about the vision and where God was taking the congregation.

Recruit Leaders

Transformational pastors and effective church planters understand that congregations grow in proportion to the recruiting, training, and releasing of leaders. This is one of the most common errors I see among many, if not most, pastors: the failure to intentionally develop leaders. A major reason for most congregations not breaking through growth barriers is that there are not enough leaders to reach and sustain growth at the next level. The most important thing I do as a pastor and a leader of a network, after casting vision, is recruiting, training, developing, and releasing leaders.

Pastors going into highly dysfunctional congregations told me that they scouted the leaders in those congregations and found no one in whom they saw great potential. They knew they needed to do two things. First, they worked with existing leaders in the congregation, who had some potential, to develop the skills they possessed, even though they knew that these leaders wouldn't be able to get them to the next level. Second, they worked hard at gathering new people and constantly scouted the ones God was sending, trying to find people with increased leadership potential. They encouraged these people to attend regularly and invited them to be part of a leadership development strategy. They usually didn't reveal their strategy; they worked with them on a relational basis and released these individuals by providing ministry opportunities.

Other pastors said that they felt there was a good corps of leaders already in place, even though they had not received intentional leadership development from other pastors. They believed their job was to recruit as many as possible to the vision while providing leadership development training and opportunities for ministry. The pastors understood that they also needed to recruit and train new leaders, but their first task was to get current leaders on board and trained for the future.

The pastors who understood the leadership issue also knew that some people (with and without leadership skills) were in leadership positions, either elected or appointed by the congregation, where they did not belong. Often a major reason that congregations are in decline or on a plateau is that the wrong people, for whatever reason, are in positions of leadership. These pastors understood that they needed from the beginning to work positively at influencing the nomination process. They began to develop strategies to do this in the first year, even if it took two to three years before the strategies were implemented.

Healthy, growing, and missional congregations develop leaders. Pastors leading change know this ongoing assignment must be addressed early on and pursued during their pastoral tenure.

Be Present in the Community

Many pastors felt it was imperative to both understand the community in which the congregation was located and be seen as a leader in the community. The first issue, learning the community, is a missional one. If a congregation is to be missional, it is imperative that leaders of the congregation understand the mission field that God has called them to reach.

All congregations deal with at least three distinct cultures. There is the national culture that in a connected world affects all of us, whether we live in a city or a rural hamlet. Generational groupings, including builders, boomers, and busters, impact all of us, regardless of location. All Americans live in a consumer-oriented culture. Most children, regardless of geographical location, are computer literate and are actively involved in social networking.

Next is the local culture, whether congregations are in a city, suburb, or small town. Every congregation is located in a microculture that shapes the values and influences of the national culture. Freeways or parks may divide the microcultures of cities, while each small town has its own history and heritage.

The last culture is that of each congregation. Its reason for being birthed, the early events that shaped its values and leaders past and present, make each congregation unique.

Pastors who unlock the doors of understanding in relation to their local cultures and lead congregations to remove barriers and build bridges to the community culture see abundant fruit for their labor.

One of our pastors moved from a rural setting in the eastern part of the United States to rural California. His only understanding of water rights was what he had seen in cowboy movies. In his new community farmers faced daily the consequences of possessing or not possessing access to water. He learned about intricate canal and drainage systems that routed water to crops and how access to that system was the difference between profit and loss for those growing food. The pastor, who led his congregation to have a motto and logo centered on living water, was told by one farmer that he, the pastor, understood the water system in the valley better than most farmers. This understanding alone gave him and his congregation status in the community and entrée into community life, opening up large doors of opportunity for spiritual and physical ministry.

Many pastors also worked hard at being visible community leaders, serving and leading their congregations to serve their communities. These factors usually resulted in increased attendance and growth, along with many becoming new disciples of Jesus Christ. These pastors developed quality relationships with many people in their communities.

Evangelize

Just as some pastors initially saw themselves, until they could re-produce leaders, as both the major connector and the first connecting system for adding people new to a congregation, others saw themselves as the primary evangelist and developer of the evangelism strategy in the congregation. Most congregations plateau or decline because the concept of mission is missing. The congregation may send dollars to missionaries, so the missionaries can do mission, but the congregation both collectively and individually does not do mission. Therefore, these pastors realized that early victories and momentum would be generated as a number of people were led to become disciples of Jesus Christ. They believed the congregation's primary mission was to make disciples and they needed to model for the congregation that such was happening.

These pastors told stories so the congregation would see how the Spirit of God was at work in bringing men and women to God through Jesus Christ. These pastors understood that new birth not only brings life to new disciples but also brings life to a dead congregation. They had the congregation celebrate the fact that God was at work in the congregation, bringing many to Jesus.

These pastors also understood that such new life encouraged many individuals in the congregation. First, it energized some to want to be a part of what God was doing. It helped the pastors raise up new leaders and servants. Second, as the pastors brought other changes that some might not like, many found it hard to speak against the changes because there was so much new life springing up throughout the congregation. Change in small, rural congregations is often in proportion to the pastor's ability to be an evangelist.

Address Money

Many pastors told me that dealing with money was a key issue that needed to be addressed up front. If the money is not available, ministry does not occur. Perhaps that was why Jesus spent so much time in his recorded ministry in the Gospels dealing with money. The use of money reflects best the hearts of people, revealing what they do and don't value, which is also why Jesus spoke so often about money. This is why in GHC we continually offer focused training for pastors and congregations on fiscal issues.

Three major issues surfaced. The first was the handling of money on a day-to-day basis. Pastors found the way money was collected, counted, and deposited, often left those doing these tasks, along with the congregation, open to loss, theft, misuse, and in some cases government penalties and fines. An early victory for some pastors was getting the monetary house in order.

The second issue was the distribution of money. How a congregation budgets and spends its money reflects collective congregational values. Often congregations value facilities over ministry, value saving money over paying servants for their labor, or value spending money on themselves rather than on conducting mission for others. A number of pastors addressed poor stewardship values and practices by dealing with budgets, financial reports, and the distribution of money given by the congregation. They understood that money is a tool for implementing the congregation's mission and doing ministry, and this tool must be used both efficiently and effectively. Wisdom is crucial.

The third and major issue was allowing people who were not financially committed to the congregation and its mission to hold leadership positions. Many pastors understood that such behavior was unwise and needed to be addressed early on. One pastor told me when he asked for the amounts that leaders (in his case the board of deacons, of which there were fifteen) gave, he was told that he didn't have access to that information. He then requested just the amounts, not the names. His evaluation of the amounts made it clear that no more than three leaders gave anything near a tithe. So he sent a letter to members of the congregation calling a special meeting to discuss what leaders gave to the church. As you can imagine, a large crowd gathered. The pastor displayed on a screen the fifteen amounts and then displayed what he and his spouse gave as a family. He told the congregation that beginning the next year, all new board deacons would have to give a more substantial proportion, or they wouldn't be nominated as deacons. He knew his approach was risky, but when the congregation saw what most gave and what he as the pastor gave, the congregation sided with him. He told me it was a key factor in determining his ability to lead the board and the congregation.

Pray

Almost all the pastors I spoke with mentioned prayer. These pastors realized that if God does not build the church of Jesus Christ, it does not get built. I put this last because in some cases the congregational culture is so rigid, the pastor is not allowed much flexibility beyond the norms of that particular culture. If such is the case, the pastor can gather a group of individuals and train them to pray for a new day. However, the pastor needs to understand that many excellent resources on prayer focus on individuals praying for individuals, not individuals praying for the congregation's ministry to the community.

The pastor should teach them to pray that God will place passion in the heart of the congregation to have a spiritual burden for lost people. The pastor can train these individuals to pray for a sense of mission and a vision for the congregation. The pastor can lead this group in prayer walks in the community to pray for specific areas of need, for individuals, and for the community at large.

Wise pastors gather around them a group of people, no matter how small, who will pray for God to lead the congregation to again be healthy, grow, and see the consistent birth of new disciples. Also, this group or another gathering of individuals needs to pray daily for the pastor and the pastor's family.

CONCLUSION

Very few pastors can do all the things listed in this chapter during their first year of ministry. However, all the pastors interviewed picked three to five of the ideas and pursued them as goals for their first year. Each pastor had an agenda, whether written or noted in the mind, and each pastor pursued that agenda with vigor. The one consistent idea was that somehow, some way, pastors took the responsibility to gather new people to the congregation. All understood the concepts of early victories, momentum, and the need for members of the congregation to see that something was occurring and new people were not only visiting the congregation but also staying. These pastors understood that it was a lost cause to seek those who had left in the past. In some cases some of those individuals returned because of what was happening in the life of the congregation. Yet the pastors knew that congregations are not built on discouraged and disgruntled folks returning, regardless of the original reason for leaving. Life and vitality come with introducing new people—and especially new believers—into congregational life.

Every pastor I spoke with also understood that the job of turning around a congregation that is on a plateau or in decline is a fifty- to sixty-hour-a week job for most weeks of the year. It is hard work that demands sacrifice. And it is not just a matter of putting in the time; it is also a matter of using that time wisely. The pastors I spoke with love their ministry calling and also love the challenge of seeing God do new things in old situations. They work hard because they know they need to but also because they love what they are doing. They are motivated by their passion for God, the church of Jesus Christ, and our Lord's mission to make disciples.

The other factor that I discovered was that they spent, on average, half of their working week in the office. Some were out of their office 60 to 70 percent of the time. Even pastors who spent large amounts of time in sermon and worship service preparation understood that they could not be in the office for great amounts of time beyond the hours spent in preparation. They were on the streets and in the community.

The first year is crucial. All wise pastors have a plan and work the plan. They work hard at establishing early victories and building momentum. Pastors also pray and get others to pray in order to ask God to bless their efforts with spiritual dynamics that only the Holy Spirit can produce.

CHAPTER 4

MONDAY: TRANSITION DAY

Emma reflected on the difference between the conference she had attended last week and the worship service yesterday. Images of people, children, songs, announcements, discussions in the parlor, and even her sermon created a kaleidoscope of thoughts. But overall she clearly understood that the congregations the conference speakers described last week were not in tune with hers, except for the congregations that were the butt of jokes and derision. It seemed as if all the mocking descriptions of dysfunctional congregations were aimed at the one over which she was the pastor.

Another problem was even more troublesome than being the pastor of "No Hope" congregation. When she left the conference, she felt empowered. The speakers talked about leadership, change, transformation, new life, and all the topics her congregation needed. And she was convinced that she could do it. She could be the leader God intended; she could motivate the congregation to change; she could deal with her "church boss" and somehow convince both him and his wife to see things her way. But now it was Monday morning and she was sitting behind her desk filled with stuff that had not been handled while she was at the conference. Her computer had a ton of e-mail, there were phone messages that needed her responses, meetings scheduled almost every night that week, and she didn't know what to do first. Worse yet she just didn't know what to do, beyond getting her desk and computer cleared, to even start to lead and see change occur. In one sense she was glad she had so much work to catch up on because if those tasks were not before her, she realized she didn't know where to even begin to see whether her congregation could become one that people bragged about at conferences rather than derided.

The tasks required to lead systemic change seemed so overwhelming and complex that Emma was almost paralyzed with confusion. Should she go after those who wanted the congregation to continue to act like it was 1950? Should she figure out what to do with the few new people who were now attending? Should she attack the bureaucracy that required meeting after meeting where nothing of significance was accomplished? Should she work on preaching brilliant sermons that would cause everyone to say, "You really know your stuff, so we will just follow your wishes for the congregation"? Should she immerse herself in more books and conferences to learn all that she now knew she didn't know? What should she do, and was there enough energy and time to see all of this happen in one lifetime? These thoughts almost made her depressed and tired. Maybe the best thing was just to keep her head down and get the day-to-day stuff done and hope that somehow, God would send her the right people who would make the congregation a different and better place to lead.

She just hoped that her "No Hope" congregation wouldn't lead her to have no hope for effective ministry.

INTRODUCTION

The Bible teaches us that Sunday is the first day of the week and Saturday is the seventh. The majority of Christians worship on Sunday as a way of celebrating the resurrection of Jesus Christ. However, for pastors in the Sunday tradition, Sunday is the last day of their workweek. Monday becomes the first day of the week, at least in practice, as wise pastors begin on Monday to prepare for Sunday.

The front door to church life for new people is no longer just Sunday worship services. Many now enter into the life and ministry of local congregations through ministry teams, small groups, service projects, or recovery ministries. Yet the majority still enter through the front door of Sunday worship. Also for those who come in through some other entrance, the focus for many is the meeting that would be described as a worship service on Sunday in congregations that meet either in buildings or in homes.

Since Sunday is still such a crucial day in congregational life, many pastors begin on Monday to gear up for the next Sunday. That makes Monday a transition day. It is the day to review and reflect on the events of Sunday and begin to plan for all that will occur during the week, leading eventually to the next Sunday worship service.

In this chapter and the following ones I discuss the optimum week in order to demonstrate key behaviors I learned from interviewing effective transformational pastors. In the previous chapter I listed a number of common denominators of these pastors as they eventually led systemic change in their congregations. I intend to show how a number of these key behaviors are reflected in pastors' actions during a week.

I want pastors to understand that this is an ideal week, and very few weeks in a pastor's life are ideal. The demands of ministry and the various individual and collective events faced by people in congregations always intrude. The biorhythms of individual pastors determine that one pastor does well in the morning and another does well in the afternoon or evening. Also, in a day when many clergy spouses work outside the home, the demands of both the congregation and the home produce different schedules. However, if no ideal is described, there is no way to measure how one's time should be used in order to model wiser ways of behaving.

In chapter 1, I laid out some parameters of the kind of pastoral family and congregational setting I'm assuming in describing such a week. Now for a few other assumptions. First, effective transformational pastors work fifty- to sixty-hour weeks at least thirty-five weeks a year. These next chapters are written from that perspective.

Second, the week is for pastors who are in their sixth or seventh month of ministry serving a new congregation. By that point, a pastor should have had time to meet and visit (in a variety of formats) with most people in the congregation. Therefore, this week does not describe initial get-acquainted visits. However, the pastors I interviewed began to implement many of the things I describe in these chapters early in their tenure with the congregation even while conducting get-acquainted visits.

Third, when pastors arrive in a new situation, it takes a while for them to shape the church calendar and the scheduling of meetings. Wise pastors shouldn't be out more than two nights a week, except when very special events are happening. Therefore, to work a minimum of fifty hours a week, they must start early in the morning and work late into the afternoon.

In this book, I have used Friday as the pastor's day off, but pastors take different days of the week as their off day. If that is the case for you, adjust the rest of the week accordingly.

BEFORE THE OFFICE OPENS: BEGINNING MINISTRY AT BREAKFAST

Breakfast and lunch are key times to meet with people in the community and to recruit and disciple leaders. If the person is not yet a disciple of Jesus Christ, the purpose of the time together is to develop a personal relationship with that individual in order to eventually introduce her or him to Jesus Christ. If the person is a leader or a potential leader in the congregation, the pastor wants not only to develop a relationship but also to disciple that individual. Therefore, these meetings during meals need to be planned and used judiciously throughout the week. In smaller communities it is crucial to find out where people gather so that the pastor may have a constant presence. Often people gather at breakfast places or coffee shops before they begin their day. The pastor should use Monday through Thursday, assuming that Friday is the pastor's day off, to eat or drink in such places and learn to act like an extrovert, even if this goes against the pastor's personal wiring. In more urban settings people may gather in one of many coffee shops that proliferate in most communities. Also, the pastor needs to develop a relationship with the workers in these establishments, whether hostess, waiter, cashier, or barista. Christians are notorious for not tipping wait staff. Leaving good tips allows us to follow our Lord's command to use money to buy spiritual influence (Luke 16:9).

It is great to be in the office before any other employees get there. Doing that models commitment and discipline, and it provides quiet time to conduct key business. Perhaps the most important thing pastors do each day is to feed their souls by having time alone with their God. Pastors need to take the lead in encouraging their flock to be in the word of God each day and in prayer. I realize there is spiritual benefit in studying the word of God for preaching; I also believe there is great spiritual benefit in reading the word of God for personal feeding and nourishment, whether or not it is ever used for teaching or preaching. Often the spirit of God speaks then about issues that may need to be addressed in the body of believers six to twelve months from the time that God teaches the pastor during his or her devotions.

Prayer time is crucial for the pastor. Obviously the pastor needs to pray for personal needs and issues and those of her or his family. The pastor also needs to pray for the congregation collectively and individually. The pastor prays for the leaders in the congregation and for the spirit of God to be at work through the pastor and others to lead change. Change pastors are developing strategies and tactics to produce change and create new health and life in the congregation. Those strategies and tactics will be effective only as the spirit of God empowers and goes before the pastor.

The pastor also needs to model personally how the pastor will train others to pray cosmically, meaning for the community and its needs. The pastor needs to pray for those with whom he or she interacts so that these individuals might cross the line of faith and become new disciples of Jesus Christ. The pastor prays for different segments (geographically, economically, socially) of the community as places the congregation will one day be able to influence spiritually. The pastor needs to pray for the mayor, town council, school superintendent, and other people in places of influence to have a personal relationship with God and also to give the congregation favor to conduct ministry in their respective areas.

The pastor as the spiritual leader of the congregation needs to lead by performing spiritual behaviors that will produce the power of the Holy Spirit in the pastor's life and in the life of the congregation. All good leaders know they cannot with integrity ask of their people what they are not willing to do. God is looking for faithful leaders who will walk the walk, not hypocrites.

MONDAY MORNING: FINISHING UP SUNDAY'S WORK

The pastor now goes through e-mail, phone, and even text messages that need responses, as well as other communication that has come into the church office from the weekend. Wise pastors don't carry their calendars with them on Sunday, or if they are in their phones, they don't refer to them since their phones are off. If people want to meet with the pastor, they are encouraged to phone, e-mail, or text requests for the pastor or administrative assistant (assuming there is such a person) to deal with on Monday. The pastor as a wise leader recognizes that it is not his or her responsibility to meet with everyone who desires a meeting. Requests are screened in order to determine why people want to meet. Leader-pastors desire to train people to meet with the person who can best meet their need, and that is not always the pastor. Often a good church secretary or administrative assistant can provide better answers than the pastor can.

Also, before the pastor agrees to meet with anyone, the pastor needs to establish his or her calendar for the week. This involves the key people who are crucial for the mission and vision. These individuals are leaders in the congregation, leaders or potential leaders the pastor is seeking to disciple in order to increase their ability to lead. The pastor also sets apart time to meet with community leaders and people outside the congregation who can help the pastor down the road see the mission and vision achieved in the community. In other words, the pastor needs to prioritize the weekly schedule in terms of how she or he is going to use the time.

If there is a secretary or administrative assistant, the pastor probably needs to meet with that person this morning and get assistance in laying out the week to protect the pastor's schedule and to delegate to others work that the pastor does not need to do personally.

By this time in the pastor's tenure, the pastor has trained the secretary or assistant in how to answer the phone and how to deal with callers. The pastor should also have a feel for how the assistant protects him or her, holds information in confidence, and whether the assistant is a source of information to other leaders in the congregation other than the pastor. It is of utmost importance to know whether this person is loyal to the pastor or more loyal to church bosses or other leaders in the tribe.

Assessing Numbers

After six months, the training of those in positions of responsibility for counting people and funds should be complete, and they should have key numbers ready for the pastor on Monday morning. The key numbers include the following:

People
Total attendance in the worship service
Breakdown of adults, children, and infants
Number of first-time guests
Number of second-time guests

Number of third-time guests
Money
Total offering
Total for general fund
Total for other key funds (building, missions, and so on)
Number of giving units that gave on Sunday
Amount of cash

All of us value different things. Whatever we value, we count. If we take four grandchildren to a theme park for the day, we count constantly. Numbers are crucial because numbers represent either people or items that are highly valued. When pastors and laity say they are not interested in numbers, they mean they don't care for people because every number represents a person. When an ocean liner or airplane goes down, following the number of people lost is the word *souls*. A headline stating that 250 souls were lost is a far more poignant statement than one that refers to 250 people.

When one realizes that money is crucial to being able to conduct effective ministry, the number of dollars becomes important. Perhaps that is one reason why Jesus spoke about money more than any other topic. The other reason is that how people spend and give their dollars determines their heart relationship with Jesus Christ.

Every transformational pastor I spoke with talked about the need to create momentum initially in order to see the congregation begin to turn around. Each of them understood that if the new pastor didn't create momentum, the leaders of the congregation, as well as the congregation itself, wouldn't regard the pastor as a leader. The first place that people see momentum is in attendance and in increased dollars. Also, most effective pastors know that while money and attendance are not the most important numbers, they are the ones that usually need to be dealt with first. The most important number is related to the number of new disciples being made for Jesus Christ. After all, the Great Commission is all about that. If there are no new people and if there are no new dollars, the congregation probably won't have many new disciples.

Effective pastors also know that as they lead change, they are likely to encounter resistance from leaders and members of the congregation. It is often more difficult to stop change if attendance and giving are up. Leaders realize that many in the congregation don't want to see the pastor's initiatives stopped because of the momentum being generated by the new pastor. Good numbers create political capital.

Some pastors tout the number of new people they have introduced to Jesus Christ and are now part of God's kingdom, but have not yet become part of the congregation. While it is good that these new individuals are part of God's kingdom, the reality is that if the congregation does not see many of them becoming part of their body, they won't see the pastor as an effective pastor. They may say the pastor is an effective evangelist, but not an effective pastor.

The Apostle Paul tells us that we are not to be lacking in zeal (Rom. 12:11). Therefore the idea of creating momentum is biblical. Leaders are zealous for God, the Lord Jesus Christ, and his church. Leaders want the church to grow (as Jesus said it would), and they want resources available to conduct effective ministry. Focusing initially on attendance and money is not a bad thing. It becomes a bad thing only when these numbers are used in a proud way to lift up the reputation of the pastor or the congregation. Sadly that is often the case, which is why emphasis on numbers has gained a poor reputation with many Christians. Often in reaction to such pride, however, believers have thrown out the baby with the bath water.

Establishing Measurables and Finding Trends

Effective pastors want to build a database of numbers that will help them track what God is doing in and through their ministries. The initial part of the database is key numbers for each Sunday of the year, which allow pastors to compare the first Sunday of this year with the first Sunday of last year. We live in a day and age when many who attend church believe that if they come two Sundays a month, they are regular in their attendance. Many congregations, including healthy and growing ones, find that attendance week to week is all across the board. The same is true with the amount of funds given each week. However, it is amazing how consistent Sundays are compared year to year.

This comparison also allows the pastor to look at trends. In many parts of the country attendance begins to build the Sunday or two after Labor Day until the Sunday before Christmas. Then it builds again the Sunday or two after the beginning of the new year until Easter. That is why pastors prefer Easter to come later in the spring. After Easter, there is a dip, and then it begins to build to Mother's Day. After Mother's Day, it declines to a summer attendance plateau.

The goal of a transformational pastor is to see the average each year go up on the comparative Sundays. Looking at comparative data for a year helps the pastor avoid the emotional highs and lows of each week. Also, an effective pastor views the Easter attendance (which is usually a congregation's highest attended day, since almost everyone who attends shows up that day) as the congregation's potential for growth. One ambitious but measurable goal is for the Easter attendance to be the average yearly attendance twelve months later.

Pastors understand that creating many Easter-type services during the year raises the average attendance. We encourage congregations to conduct several big events on Sundays throughout the year as a way to have "more Easters" in terms of attendance.

The pastor studies the attendance and giving numbers on Monday morning and builds a flow chart for comparison for years to come. Many smaller congregations don't do this, which is why this is often the pastor's responsibility until the pastor can train someone to put together the data each week.

Connecting with Visitors

After finishing with numbers, the pastor focuses on connecting with visitors who attended as first-, second-, or third-time guests.

Remember that in early turnaround situations, the pastor is not only the key networker connecting new people to the congregation; the pastor is also the entire connector system.

Congregations deal with four mission fields. The first mission field is the people who show up on Sunday. This includes people who attend regularly but are not yet disciples of Jesus Christ, and guests or visitors. In all congregations, but especially mainline congregations, there are some who attend regularly and are probably members but are not yet disciples of Jesus Christ. I have heard too many stories in GHC, with its strong American Baptist connections, of longtime members who have made a profession of faith in Jesus Christ recently because they intentionally were asked to describe where they were in the spiritual pilgrimage with God and Jesus Christ. That is often the case with first-time guests, even if these individuals already hold membership in another congregation.

This first mission field is the easiest and least expensive to reach since these people are on the congregation's campus and have come to you. Strangely this is often the most ignored mission field. I continue to be amazed at how little attention is paid to first-time guests, encouraging them to return, become a disciple, and become an integral part of the congregation.

Effective pastors make sure that each Sunday, guests are welcomed, and each guest, member, and attendee is encouraged to fill out the attendee's card. Often guests are offered incentives to complete these cards. This is one way to take attendance, though counting is crucial since at the most only 80 percent of people will fill out cards. It is also a way to obtain prayer requests and learn of other needs in the congregation. Plus it enables the pastor to learn who are first-, second-, or third-time guests.

Many first-time guests won't fill out cards. The advantage of being in a smaller congregation is that usually the pastor, by six months into the process, knows which people are visitors. Now, this assumes that on Sunday morning the pastor is not in the pastor's office but is out with the congregation exercising leader care and keeping an eye open for visitors. When the pastor meets visitors, he or she should ask questions that elicit insight into them and where they live.

On Monday morning, the pastor reviews cards and other sources of information, often coming from the pastor's connection the day before with new people, before welcoming and thanking them for their attendance. Wise pastors contact those individuals by phone, e-mail, text, Facebook, or other means while allowing people the freedom not to respond if they choose to maintain a level of anonymity. Also, wise pastors recognize that second- and third-time guests are indicating enough interest to return, reflecting some desire to see how the congregation might minister to their needs. These pastors have thought through how to respond in an appropriate way and have a strategy in place to invite them to take next steps leading to greater commitment and involvement.

One of the most effective ways for the pastor to connect with first-time visitors is to invite them to lunch next week after the service. The pastor and the congregation then have two attempts to serve these individuals and meet some of their initial felt needs. The pastor can connect with these individuals, learn more about them, and share the vision of the congregation. Most important, if two or more guests from different families accept the invitation to lunch, the pastor can connect them with each other.

The bottom line is that a major task on Monday morning is to be the connecting system until the pastor can train leaders to serve in this crucial area.

Review

The next item on the pastor's agenda, before or after lunch, is to review Sunday and all that occurred. The pastor needs to touch base with those working the parking lot and helping older people, single mothers, disabled persons, and guests into the facilities. The pastor needs to review what she or he personally observed regarding how guests and others were greeted and treated before entering the main worship space. The pastor needs to review how guests were seated and what took place in the main worship space before the service began.

The next major piece for review is the worship service from the time it started until it finished. The critique should note what occurred and what didn't happen that perhaps should have. Here are some questions to ask:

- Did the service flow well?

- Was there much dead air time between the elements and those who participated?

- Did the service move toward a conclusion?

- Was the music appropriate?

- Was the service guest friendly? (Would people who usually don't go to church feel as though they were included in what was happening?)

- How were announcements handled?

- Did the media add to or distract from the worship experience?

- Did the service possess large-group dynamics?

- Did the service run on time?

- Was the service "lost conscious" (that is, communicating well to the spiritual needs of unbelievers)?

Obviously not all problems can be fixed at once. But if the pastor is concerned not only about curb appeal but also about worship dynamics, the pastor needs to evaluate and work on each piece of the entire worship experience during the first year. If someone can record the service, the pastor can see how it looked from the back of the worship center, not up front where most pastors are during services.

Listening to the sermon to hear how the pastor communicated is helpful. Are people actually listening? The pastor should also pay attention to how people with little or no church background responded to the sermon.

The pastor should review what occurred after the service. For example, did the pastor have another opportunity to speak with new people, and if not, why not? The pastor may want to write a critique of each Sunday, stating what worked well and what needs improvement. The pastor then decides the issues that can be addressed in the immediate future and those that may need to be addressed later on.

The wise pastor uses lunchtime to meet with an unbeliever, a person in the community who may open up a door of service for the congregation down the road, or a leader the pastor is in the process of training.

MONDAY AFTERNOON: ORGANIZATION AND PLANNING

After lunch, the pastor needs to spend the rest of the day in organization and planning. Perhaps the best thing to do first is to catch up on phone and text messages and e-mails that can be answered quickly and succinctly. Part of being seen as a credible leader is staying on top of communication. The more quickly these kinds of things can be turned around, the better it serves the pastor and the reputation the pastor is attempting to build with people who are yet to see the pastor as a leader.

On Monday the pastor also deals with organizational issues that relate to anticipated systemic changes and special events on the near horizon. For example, most pastors need to address financial stewardship in some way. If the leaders of the congregation see the pastor as the real spiritual leader, they recognize that the pastor can be trusted with knowing how much individuals in the congregation give annually. After all if they trust the pastor to handle the word of God week after week, they can surely trust the pastor with this information. However, many congregations don't trust the pastor and have baptized as a spiritual right the ungodly American value that what I give is private business. In that case the pastor should at least be able to see the amounts from individual giving units. In most smaller congregations, 10 to 20 percent of givers provide 50 to 70 percent of the congregation's income. Very few people give 10 percent. Most American Christians tip God rather than obey the biblical command about giving in a sacrificial way.

One way to increase stewardship is to thank people for their giving on a quarterly basis. By doing this, the pastor reminds them of the amount that has been donated to date and shares how financial gifts are being turned into spiritual investments. Each quarterly letter includes a story of someone who has become a new disciple of Jesus Christ or has been ministered to in a significant way. It provides a way to gracefully ask people to increase their giving in light of how God is using money to increase and develop ministry effectiveness in the congregation. It enables the pastor to increase the sense of momentum as those who attend read about all that God is doing in the lives of the congregation and in the community.

Another possible task during the afternoon is to evaluate the materials given to people when they enter the facilities on Sunday. In this day of computers, when creating and reproducing printed material is fairly easy and inexpensive to do, continual change is both good and realistic. For example, many pastors change the card they ask people to fill out each Sunday in order to find what works best. What format obtains the most responses and provides the best data?

The pastor may also develop invitation cards that people in the congregation can use to invite other individuals to church for a special preaching series, a big event, or another outreach endeavor.

Monday is not just the day to deal with the organizational issues related to Sunday and the normal business of the week. It is also the day to deal with organizational issues related to upcoming events. A wise pastor is thinking ahead and laying groundwork for these events. Also, the pastor is preparing a list of people, with varying skills and talents, who might assist with these events.

The pastor has two more items to accomplish on Monday afternoon. The next to last item relates to the continual casting of vision. The pastor is the keeper of the mission and the caster of the vision. This task takes on greater significance when the pastor has come to a congregation in decline or on a plateau. The mission for such a congregation is to be the custodian of the saints, and that mission is not going to be changed easily or quickly. The pastor must constantly deal with the mission (the purpose for which the congregation exists) and the vision (a picture of a changed community because the mission has been implemented well). A key ingredient is to constantly cast a vision that will one day occur because the mission of the congregation has changed.

Wise pastors also know that people are not open to a new vision if their choice is a new vision (a preferable future) versus the status quo (that which is known and comfortable, even if it is leading to eventual death). People are open to a new vision only when the status quo is unacceptable. For example, a heart attack does much more to motivate overweight people to change their eating habits than any number of lectures, advertisements, television shows, teachings on diabetes, and loss of mobility. The experience of a heart attack makes the status quo unacceptable, and a vision of a newer, slimmer self becomes more engaging. If casting vision is a 24/7 task, creating urgency for the vision is also a 24/7 job.

Pastors on Monday need to plan how to communicate the vision and urgency for the vision in next Sunday's worship service. The urgency and vision are to be articulated in a variety of ways all fifty-two Sundays a year, even if the pastor is on vacation. It is that crucial. On Monday the pastor needs to plan how it will be done and find resources, if necessary, to do it well. An example might be announcing before the offering that fifteen elementary-age children were in Sunday school last week, filling the current room to maximum capacity. Then thank the people for their giving, asking them to pray that God will supply the funds to redecorate a larger room for children as the Sunday school continues to grow. (I have provided a month of examples in the appendix of my book *Direct Hit*.)

The final item on the pastor's to-do list is to spend the last hour to half hour of the day, say 4:00 to 5:00 P.M., attending to self-development as a leader. This may entail reading books or articles on leadership. It may mean checking out key blogs or websites written by other effective pastor-leaders. The pastor can accomplish it in various ways, but he or she needs to be intentional about doing it and approach the learning in a systematic way. For example, listening to books on CD while driving is an effective way to be exposed to key books. The pastor who is not developing herself or himself as a leader won't be able to take the congregation to the levels of effectiveness that the mission of Jesus Christ requires.

Doing this last means the pastor will do it while tired, which is not always best. However, saving it until last means the pastor goes home with new and exciting ideas permeating his or her thoughts at the end of a long day.

MONDAY EVENING

This schedule assumes that the pastor has no meetings on Monday night. If that is not the case, the schedule would change as I demonstrate in the chapters on Tuesday and Wednesday when the pastor has evening responsibilities.

Working from 7:00 A.M. to 5:00 P.M., including breakfast and lunch times, is a long day. (I'm assuming the pastor discussed the schedule with lay leaders before coming to the congregation.) Setting boundaries is important. When the pastor works, the pastor works, and when the pastor is home, the pastor is home. The spouse, if there is one and he or she is able, should run interference for phone calls, and the pastor needs to be disciplined enough to ignore e-mail and text messages. The only calls that should be taken would be from people new to the congregation responding to invitations from the pastor for future meetings and one or two key leaders in the congregation. Even so, the pastor needs to establish an appointment for a future phone call or a face-to-face meeting with these individuals rather than conduct work while at home.

At home the pastor should spend quality time with her or his spouse and family. The pastor may need to negotiate with her or his spouse the downtime required to be alone and to reenergize.

CONCLUSION

I'm sure many readers may feel tired after reviewing the schedule I have laid out. If so, consider three things. First, planting a new congregation or turning around a congregation that has been on a plateau or in decline for several years is not for the fainthearted. It demands hard work. Also, pastors who think that people are going to follow them simply because they are the pastor are quite mistaken. Even those who say they will follow won't do that over the long term if followership is simply demanded or expected.

Second, if Jesus has called us to lead a missional entity, Jesus has called us to a challenging task that requires much prayer, hard work, patience, and a willingness to face loss and often great reward. Real pastors are women and men of grace and compassion who, like our Lord, underneath are tenacious, steadfast, relentless, and committed to tough challenges because we love our God and we love people enough to want God's best for them.

Third, if we love our jobs, the demands I have laid out are ones we relish. True leaders want to see the mission of God accomplished. They want to see people motivated to serve in sacrificial ways. They want to see the kingdom of God advance. God is looking for velvet-covered bricks who seek to serve their Savior by leading his servants to accept the mission and be willing to serve at all costs.*

---

* Please check Appendix 2 to see how to convince your congregational leaders to reimburse you for meal expenses related to your meetings with people for breakfast and lunch.

MONDAY

7:00 A.M.	Have a key breakfast (with an unbeliever, a potential leader or a community leader)
8:00-9:00 A.M.	Have a quiet time with God in Scripture reading and prayer
9:00-11:30 A.M.	Check on communications from the week end
	Establish the pastor's weekly schedule of meetings
	Meet with the administrative assistant or church secretary
	Work with attendance and giving numbers and evaluate yearly data base
	Contact first, second and third time guests
	Begin the review of Sunday including the worship service and the sermon
11:30 A.M.-1:00 P.M.	Have lunch with an unbeliever, leader or community person
1:00-5:00 P.M.	Continue review of Sunday if needed
	Catch up on messages that can be handled quickly
	Review organizational tasks for systemic change and future events
	Develop urgency and vision pieces for next Sunday's worship
	Spend time on self-development as a leader
5:00 P.M. to Bedtime	Set aside a quiet time with God in Scripture reading and prayer. Spend time with family

CHAPTER 5

TUESDAY: PREPARATION DAY

Derek realized he had been staring at the wall for fifteen minutes, and the open screen on his computer was still blank. He was tempted to go back and check e-mail for the third time in the last half hour. Bored with solitaire, he knew that looking at e-mail or playing games was just a diversion keeping him away from his sermon prep. He thought back to seminary, being excited about taking homiletics. The thought of standing in front of people and sharing a word from God to a congregation filled with anticipation, waiting to hear him speak, caused shivers to run up and down his arms. But that was more than a decade ago, and the image from seminary was not his consistent reality.

He was now preaching to his third congregation in ten years. He had been the pastor here longer than in his previous two charges. He had preached all of the sermons he felt were worth repeating. Every Sunday now was new material. He could not imagine how people who wrote for newspapers daily or magazines regularly did it time after time for years. He had forty to forty-five deadlines a year, depending on vacation and guest preachers, and he was constantly stymied, looking for good material. He knew he had improved since seminary, but that didn't produce much satisfaction since he now understood how poorly he had preached then. The drive was gone, his creativity was lacking, and if he was honest, he was often bored listening to himself preach.

Even worse, he was not sure that he was making any real difference in the lives of those who attended every week. Sometimes at funerals he felt he had offered comfort to the bereaved through his preaching, but real-life change for individuals busy with their families, careers, and advancement didn't seem to happen much, if at all. Some people told him how his sermons helped them, and for that he was grateful, but these people never seemed to be the ones that the rest of the congregation looked up to as either leaders in the congregation or high achievers in life.

In down times like these Derek also thought of the stewardship issue. On average seventy people gave up a half hour of their time to listen to him each week. It was not the same seventy each week, but it was seventy people nonetheless. That was thirty-five people hours every week. Often, he was convinced he was wasting their time on most Sundays. He was tired of using the same format week after week, he was tired of stating the platitudes that often seemed so trite, he was tired of watching the young people in the back texting while he was speaking, and he was just plain tired of trying to come up with a meaningful sermon week after week.

Derek had been around congregations enough to know that his days with this one were probably being numbered. He did not know how to lead, and he realized that most were tired of listening to him preach each week and were ready for a change. He had to admit that his dreams in seminary of seeing lives changed from his speaking had become personal nightmares. He looked at his watch. Another fifteen minutes had gone by, and the computer screen was still blank.

INTRODUCTION

I have had a long infatuation with preaching. When I was five, I would come home from church, set up the piano stool in the living room, put my Bible on it, and preach. My sermons produced amusement and then boredom as I kept saying the same things over and over, just louder. I possess enough of that memory to recall that I mostly shouted and told the imaginary crowd how bad they were. I preached my first sermon in our church when I was fifteen and realized that all the material I had studied took only fifteen minutes to say. After taking homiletics in Bible college, I went to seminary and for the first time was confronted with a person who not only preached well but also really understood oral communication. That person was Haddon Robinson. Preaching then moved from being a biblical or exegetical lecture to a persuasive speech about God and God's revelation to those God had created in his image, based on solid biblical study. I have now preached most Sundays for more than forty years in vocational ministry and taught homiletics at the baccalaureate, master's, and doctoral levels. I have had the privilege of teaching with Haddon and spending many hours discussing the art of narrative preaching with him. I taught for many years in the Schuller School for preachers and continue to teach in DMin courses. I love to preach, I love to hear good preachers, and I love to teach others to preach well.

Having said all this, I believe that for the average pastor, preaching in our nation has fallen on bad times. I find most preachers boring, and in many cases I would get up and leave in the middle of their sermons, except that would send too many discouraging signals to the preachers and the congregations. I also believe we have created a large population of churchgoers who are spiritual masochists; they have been so beaten up by boring and irrelevant preachers that anything good in a sermon causes them to rejoice over the greatness of their particular preacher. I also believe that in congregations that view themselves as custodians of saints, their particular sermon style is as absolute as the Scriptures themselves. Any preacher who can preach well in that particular tradition is applauded more for fitting into the tradition than for communicating in a relevant way.

The other issue contributing to the current situation is that many pastors are poorly trained in communication (homiletics) and don't work at their craft. As a result, they often spend the minimum amount of time on preaching and don't have a burning desire to hone their skills. The result is uncreative and irrelevant sermons that bore the congregation. Yet many congregations won't say this openly because doing so seems unspiritual. In some cases if the pastor is beloved for meeting needs within the congregation, the pastor is given a pass as a preacher, and her or his communication sins are forgiven.

Good leader-pastors understand the power of the pulpit. Where else do people voluntarily give up their time to listen to someone speak uninterrupted for twenty to forty minutes? Casting vision on a one-to-one basis is good and necessary, yet far more can be accomplished when the leader can do it with the whole group time after time. Laying out the theological and practical urgency for the mission and vision is also accomplished much more effectively when it can be done on a consistent basis with a group of people. Stories of how God is working to implement the mission and achieve the vision have more power when a group can hear the story all at once. If the church of Jesus Christ is a missional entity, leader-pastors are constantly living, speaking, and behaving with a persuasive stance in all they do. No other place fits this act of persuasion better than the pulpit, where the leader is given the opportunity to persuade from God's perspective, correctly using God's revelation as the authority.

ASSUMPTIONS

Tuesday is the day the pastor prepares to preach. Before reading about what the pastor does in terms of preparation and how it is to be done, consider some assumptions:

One Good Sermon a Week

Busy pastors, particularly those leading transformation, can produce only one good message or lesson a week in light of all their other responsibilities. Some pastors may preach or teach more often than once most weeks, but they can prepare for only one excellent presentation.

Our Authority

The only authority that any preacher has to ask anyone or any congregation to change is the word of God. Therefore the study of God's word is crucial for any sermon since it must be the basis for what the pastor asks the congregation to believe and, in light of that belief, how one is to live.

Persuasion

All good preaching at its heart is persuasion. This takes on greater meaning if the pastor believes the church of Jesus Christ is a missional entity. God is calling us to live and act individually and collectively to achieve the mission that Jesus Christ gave to his church.

Speaking as People Listen

People live, learn, and listen inductively, but because most preachers are taught to preach deductively, most preachers preach contrary to how people learn and listen. Learning to preach inductively is crucial if people are first going to hear and then act on what they hear.

Stories

God's number one way of revealing truth in Scripture is through story and narrative. People learn and are motivated best through story. This truth takes on even greater significance in a culture saturated by media and the use of story. Preachers need to embrace and use the concept of story and then tell stories, tell stories, and tell more stories. Making moral pronouncements and imposing guilt don't work and produce passive resistance.

Creativity

Creativity in communicating demands time. Most preachers are not creative because they don't devote enough time to their preparation. However, this time can be generated without adding to the number of hours the pastor spends in preparation.

Sermon Development

The preparation of sermons involves two aspects: the study that is the basis for what is said, and the development of what is studied for presentation. Good speakers spend equal amounts of time on each aspect.

TUESDAY MORNING: STUDY

The pastor again starts the day at 7:00 A.M. with a breakfast meeting designed either to engage people to become disciples of Jesus Christ or to recruit and/or train individuals in the congregation in leadership.

The pastor then spends time in private devotions. One element that is added to the pastor's prayer list is the request that Holy Spirit provide insight during the study of the word of God in preparing the sermon.

The pastor asks the assistant or church secretary to hold all calls until after lunch since the pastor needs to spend quality time in the study. When I was a solo pastor, on a regular basis I asked the people during the Sunday morning worship hour not to call the office in the morning, unless there was an emergency, since I had no secretary. I told them that I was using that time to prepare to preach on Sunday, and the need to be uninterrupted was crucial to how well I preached on Sunday. I was amazed that the majority of people in the congregation honored that request. My request also let the congregation know that I was taking preaching seriously and that I wanted to honor and respect their time each Sunday morning by preaching better each week.

The pastor then spends the next four to five hours conducting research into sermon preparation. The only break is for a meaningful lunch with a key individual.

Almost every transformational pastor I interviewed possessed a preaching plan for the first six to twelve months. These plans were designed to lay the biblical, theological, and practical groundwork for the changes they would be leading the congregation to embrace. Many plans included several series of sermons that covered at least the first six months of Sundays, if not the entire year. Key subjects mentioned by many pastors were related to the missional nature of the kingdom of God, the missional nature of the church, the church in action as revealed in the book of Acts, and the responsibilities of believers, both individually and collectively, to be making disciples and modeling the love of God through compassion and mercy ministries. These pastors understood that each sermon was not going to change minds, behaviors, and attitudes that would move the congregation from an inward focus to an outward one. However, they realized that these things needed to be said initially so that in many conversations, the pastor could refer to them to demonstrate why he or she was acting in certain ways and was encouraging the congregation to behave in certain ways. The goal was to change the conversations so that eventually beliefs and behaviors would change.

The Creative Cycle

Most pastors lack creativity in preaching because they allow too little time between their work of study and their work of determining how they will communicate what they have studied. Many pastors are diligent about doing their study early in the week, and then near the end of the week they put it together to be ready to preach on Sunday. That leaves only three or four days for the material that has been studied to simmer in their brains and for pastors to find material to aid in communication.

I teach and encourage preachers to use the creative cycle. That is, the pastor studies on a Tuesday for a sermon that will be preached twelve days later on a Sunday. The pastor then has nine to ten days between the study of the material and the design of how to communicate it. This process does not require more time in preparation, but it does require the pastor to be disciplined to study each week, whether the pastor is preaching that Sunday or not.

The creative cycle does several things for communicators. First, it gives the mind time to understand the material that has been studied, even to the point of perceiving how it needs to be organized both for understanding and for persuasion. I was always amazed at the clarity of understanding that emerged when I would come back the second week and look at what I studied the previous week. Many questions and difficulties that arose in my study were somehow resolved and made sense. Also, I understood the passage's meaning and intent far more clearly when I came back to the text.

Second, the creative cycle prompts a continual stream of resources for support material. Conversations, items in books and articles, snippets from media presentations, and everyday behaviors pastors experience in personal and family life, as well as the lives of others, become potential resources for communicating the material.

Third, nine to ten days later creativity in the pastor's mind guides him or her to ways to organize and present the material so that it will generate and maintain interest with the audience and achieve the pastor's purpose.

All good preaching involves clarity, persuasion, and change. Through the grace of God, the pastor seeks change in the understanding of people, the beliefs of people, and the behavior of people. Such change does not happen if people don't listen, are not engaged, and don't find the material relevant to their life situations. All sermon preparation involves content, the organization of the content, the editing of the content (what one leaves out and what one includes), and the presentation of the content in ways that are meaningful for listeners. The creative cycle enables the communicator to come to the preparation of the material with far more material than can be used. The preacher seldom is looking for the final concluding story, the right illustration, or the best way to get started. The creative cycle allows the pastor to have multiple choices of material along with multiple options of presentation.

When I taught homiletics at the seminary level, I was preaching to the same congregation each Sunday for most of the year. I was also running the seminary's DMin program while completing a PhD degree. I found that preaching well each week to the same three congregations was impossible without using the creative cycle. In my case, the process was study on Monday or Tuesday and put the sermon together on Saturday. If I preached poorly on Sunday, I wasted time for more than eight hundred people. My sense of responsibility for the stewardship God had given me meant that I needed to employ the creative cycle to present God's message week after week as well as I possibly could.

The Study

I hope that all pastors begin their study with the word of God. Some may start with the passages in the lectionary, others may look at passages related to the topic or theological tenet they wish to cover in the sermon, and still others may start with a passage of scripture, particularly if they are preaching through a book of the Bible. In any case, if our authority is the word of God, it is crucial to study God's word in some depth. I also hope that pastors spend quality time in the study of the word in order to understand the biblical writer's intent in writing this particular passage or passages. Pastors may then move on to historical, archeological, and sociological materials that relate to the passage or topic. Knowing what others, with greater background and experience than most pastors, have said about this passage, topic, or theological tenet is important.

Over the years I have identified several issues that are fundamental to the study process. First, we need to write out as much as possible the thoughts and ideas we are wrestling with in our study. Writing out our ideas, even though we may not want to take the time and may be tempted not to write out precisely what we are discovering, produces accuracy while forcing us to examine our thinking and our logic. Many sermons I hear are filled with poor thinking as well as poor logical development. Often this lack of clarity and preciseness begins with the pastor's lack of discipline in writing while he or she studies.

Second, all communicators agree, regardless of the content of the communication, that we can communicate only one idea at a time. Advertisers spend millions of dollars on advertising campaigns to communicate one idea for each of their products. Writers of screenplays for movies and television, as well as directors of the dramas, understand that each work communicates one basic idea. And yet most preachers communicate a myriad of ideas in twenty to forty minutes of preaching.

Third, we need to create an outline using complete sentences. This kind of outline forces us to see whether our ideas (since each sentence is a separate idea) go together, separate the primary ideas from supportive ones, and determine how all the ideas in the outline fit the main idea to be communicated at some point in the future.

The Goal

By the time the pastor finishes her or his study, either before going to lunch with a key person or soon after returning from lunch, the goal is to have a completed sentence outline that clearly explains the main idea of the sermon. The outline is extensive enough that someone who does not know what the pastor has been studying could look at it and understand intellectually the topic about which the pastor will be preaching in twelve days. The main idea is written in the form of a timeless theological proposition. At this point the pastor should be able to stand in front of the congregation and communicate the material as a lecture informing them of the idea, how the idea comes from Scripture, and why that idea is of valid consideration for their lives, purely from an intellectual perspective. The bottom line is a clear presentation of the biblical idea that will be preached.

To create such a document, the pastor must ask three functional questions of the text or texts upon which the passage is based. In a sense these questions are asked by any communicators, of the audience being addressed, including the biblical writers. Here are the three questions:

- Does the audience need to understand this idea?

- Does the audience need to believe this idea?

- Do people in the audience need to implement this idea in their lives?

All communicators deal with one, two, or all three questions every time they interact with an audience. The biblical writers were no different. They, too, were writing to communicate God's ideas to their audiences.

The first question deals with ignorance. The communicator assumes the audience is ignorant of a certain truth and writes to provide the information to remedy the ignorance. The second question deals with persuasion. Just because people know a truth does not mean they believe it. The writer persuades people to believe. The third question relates to behavior. The Bible is quite clear that sin is knowing, believing, and not behaving accordingly. The writer urges people to act on what they know and believe.

An excellent example is found in 1 Corinthians 8–10. The Corinthian believers asked Paul about whether it was proper to eat meat that pagans offered to idols.

The Apostle Paul started with his main idea about how to deal with this issue. He stated that knowledge about the issue made Christians proud, and therefore they should exercise love. In chapter 8 he explained this thesis, thereby answering the first functional question. He ended that chapter by saying he loved brothers and sisters so much that he would never eat meat again if that was what it took. He knew he must convince believers to believe his thesis, and so from 9:1 through 10:13 he wrote a defense of his thesis, attempting to persuade, thereby answering the second functional question. Beginning in 10:14 through the end of the chapter, he demonstrated how this belief is to be lived out in action, thereby answering the third functional question.

When I'm finished this Tuesday, my goal is to have a clear statement of the idea, an extended sentence outline of how to explain the idea, and an answer to the first functional question by clearly explaining the idea using the outline I have developed. I'm convinced that once I can explain clearly, twelve days later, I will have the creative wherewithal to explain it, prove it, and demonstrate its implementation. Once I accomplish this, I put the material away and won't look at it again until Thursday of next week.

There is one other key element to using the creative cycle. While the pastor is studying the material for the sermon twelve days away, the pastor must be disciplined to focus only on the understanding of the material being studied, not the way to communicate the material. The pastor must build a mental wall between what occurs on Tuesday and what occurs on Thursday a week later, when the pastor takes out the material and begins to develop the sermon. This requires both discipline and practice since it is a very real temptation, while studying, to think about how to preach the material. However, such thought will impede the pastor's ability to understand the material being studied and gain clarity. It will also shape the pastor's thoughts, leading to the poor exegesis of texts and the illogical development of material.

TUESDAY LUNCH: CIVIC CONNECTIONS

Most pastors interviewed shared that they joined a civic organization as soon as they arrived in a new community. The majority got involved with the Chamber of Commerce or Rotary. The primary reason was that these two organizations had a feel for the entire community and what was happening currently and what was going to be happening in the future.

Many pastors functioned as extroverts, even if that was not their natural wiring. They wanted to meet key civic leaders in order to develop ongoing relationships with them and with other key businesspeople in the community. Many pastors were intentional about getting involved so that they would be seen not as ones who were just there to gain but as ones who wished to give back. They also understood that the more they were involved, the more good relationships they would be able to foster for use down the road in having their congregation serve the community.

All the pastors I interviewed assured me that meetings with key leaders in the community eventually enabled their congregations to become significant players in ministering effectively to the community. Their congregations gained excellent reputations as serving organizations that helped meet key social and economic problems faced by their respective communities.

Since Tuesday is a study day, and such meetings may demand more time for lunch, the pastor may need to start earlier in the morning to accomplish all that needs to be done on this day.

TUESDAY AFTERNOON: PREPARATION

The pastor has to do two other things before leaving early, between 3:00 and 3:30 P.M. The reason the pastor is leaving early is that the monthly board or council meeting is held at 7:00 P.M.

First, the pastor works on the Sunday morning worship service. Yesterday the pastor thought through how to communicate the vision

105

and urgency for the vision on Sunday. These communication events might take place during the call to worship; the announcements; the children's story, if there is one; the comments before the offering; or the sermon. The pastor also works on the dynamics of the Sunday morning worship service. Perhaps there are certain songs the pastor wants the congregation to sing, a responsive reading, or a faith story that someone will share with the congregation. All of this needs to be laid out so the pastor can make sure that people are being contacted in order to plan and prepare for their roles. People leading the service need to know what is happening so they, too, can prepare.

By the time the pastor completes this task, he or she has created a list of the people who need to be contacted by certain times so that the worship service may go as well as possible. In early turnaround situations these key issues cannot be delegated for someone else to plan and implement. The pastor may ask the assistant or secretary to contact people and the worship people to rehearse their parts; however, the pastor needs to be both the director and the producer for the worship service.

Second, the pastor plans the leadership training that he or she will give the first thirty to forty-five minutes of the board or council meeting. The pastor came to the congregation with the expectation of this training time, and it has been done at every meeting. Also, by this time, the pastor should have a good relationship with the board chair and should know everything that will be on the agenda so that nothing unexpected will be brought up at the meeting. If any board member in the meeting brings up something unexpected, the pastor and board chair understand that such issues won't be discussed at this meeting but will be carried over to a later one.

At this point the pastor goes home for a few hours and a meal. The pastor needs to spend this time with the family.

TUESDAY EVENING

Wise pastors realize that when they come to lead a new congregation, they are not viewed as leaders, regardless of their background or experience. They also understand that a major part of becoming the leader is leading the formal structure of the organization. (By the way, wise pastors also know they need to learn the informal structure of the congregation and eventually lead that as well.)

The first way the pastor begins to establish leadership is to provide leadership training for the board or council. This material needs to be relevant to the leaders, to their roles, and more important, to their lives outside the congregation. When the teacher can add benefit to those being taught, that person gains in the ability to influence, which is what leadership really is. Also someone who teaches well gains status with those he or she teaches. This is why effective preaching is so important.

The second way the pastor gains influence with the board is to demonstrate competency in fulfilling the role of pastor. This is again why momentum is so important. Most pastors want and are given a time to report. The pastor should use this report time to demonstrate the momentum that is occurring. Early on the pastor may feel like the wizard behind the curtain, turning wheels and keeping things moving. However, as time goes by and board or council members see new people attending, see income increasing, and hear stories of transformed lives, they, too, begin to sense the momentum. It is also crucial during this early time for these leaders to hear that the responsibilities they expect the pastor to fulfill are being met. This is one reason the pastor works much harder during the initial transformation of the congregation than later, when new systems are in place.

The third way to gain influence with this formal leadership group is to develop relationships on a personal level. This is where breakfast and lunch meetings are helpful. During these personal interactions, the pastor learns about the people, their interests, successes, needs, and desires for themselves and for their families. Next, the pastor invites them to share their passions, where they would like to see God work, and even perhaps use the congregation to make a difference in their community. Then, the pastor feels them out about their commitment to an outward-focused mission and vision. Finally, the pastor explores whether they will be open to meeting for personal and individual training as a leader. It is crucial early on to gauge people's response to the pastor as a person and leader, and to the mission and vision, including those that dislike the new direction (for a whole variety of reasons, most of which have nothing to do with the leadership at all).

The fourth way to gain influence is to act like a leader when he or she is with people, individually and collectively. The pastor needs to take an interest in what is discussed, whether the pastor cares about the topics or not. Most boards and councils are not going to let the pastor run the meetings initially unless that is the congregation's or denomination's particular tradition. That does not mean the pastor remains quiet. It also means that the pastor doesn't dominate the meeting. A leader-pastor is strong but not dominating. A leader-pastor prays for and demonstrates wisdom in when to speak and when to be quiet. A leader-pastor constantly brings the conversation back to the mission and vision of the congregation.

Wise pastors develop the best possible relationship with the board or council chairperson. Usually this person does not see the pastor as the leader, regardless of what he or she might say to the contrary. Also this person is usually part of the congregation's informal power structure or at least strongly influenced by those who are part of that structure. If such is the case, the pastor needs to at least develop a relationship of honesty and fair play, which means letting the pastor know what is on the agenda rather than being blindsided in meetings. Also, pastors should recognize that when the council has more than ten people on it, the key decisions are not made at the meetings; they are made ahead of time in parking lots, at golf courses or bowling alleys, over meals, and through e-mail or phone conversations between two or three key influencers and their spouses. Godly leaders are wise like serpents while being harmless as doves. They must also remember that they are in the meeting primarily to represent Jesus Christ and his mission for the church.

After each board or council meeting, the pastor should retire to the office to review the meeting. The pastor should reflect on what happened, how it happened, and why individuals spoke or voted as they did. The pastor also needs to make a list of things that must be done and people who need to be contacted to leverage for God and the mission those things that did or didn't happen in the meeting.

CONCLUSION

Tuesday is primarily the first of two days of preparation for the preaching event during the Sunday worship service. I'm assuming that pastors need to spend a minimum of eight to ten hours preparing for Sunday, and this preparation needs to be done in two halves on two separate days. Preachers need to spend more time in preparation, but many may not. Pastors who spend more time will reap greater rewards and see change occur more quickly. However, I'm convinced that eight to ten hours are more than most pastors spend in getting ready for Sunday.

Pastors who prepare in this manner employ the creative cycle, which puts nine to ten days between the pastor's study and the preparation for communicating what the pastor has learned in study. The creative cycle does not require more time in preparation, but it does require the discipline to separate the study of material from the organization of that material to preach.

Pastors then take time to think through Sunday's worship service. They determine what needs to happen and who is responsible for making it happen as well as the individuals who will actually implement the plan, if they are different people. The pastor acts as both the producer (determining who does what) and the director (scripting the order, as much as possible this early in the pastor's tenure) of the worship service.

The pastor also uses Tuesday to prepare for a key meeting that evening, which is the monthly meeting with those who make up the formal structure of the congregation. Obviously if such key meetings occur at other times, the pastor will adjust accordingly.

TUESDAY

7:00-8:00 A.M.	Have breakfast with a key person.
8:00-9:00 A.M.	Have a devotional time.
9:00-Noon	Study for the sermon twelve days away.
Noon-1:00 P.M.	Attend civic organization lunch meeting.
1:00-2:00 P.M.	Continue study.
2:00-3:00 P.M.	Work on key things that need to happen in the Sunday worship service. Prepare for the board or council meeting.
4:00-7:00 P.M.	Be home.
7:00-9:00 P.M.	Meet with board.

CHAPTER 6

WEDNESDAY: COMMUNITY DAY

Todd had just finished helping wash all the dishes. He now sat alone in the church Fellowship Hall that recently was filled with many of the poor and homeless people in the community. Every Wednesday morning, he along with six to eight others fed forty to fifty people, depending on the weather and other variables he wasn't quite sure he knew or understood. As he put his feet up on a chair and drank his coffee, he realized he had mixed emotions about this ministry of the congregation.

On the one hand, he had a great sense of satisfaction and fulfillment in seeing hungry people helped. This feeling was intensified when he saw the eyes of young children light up as they heaped their trays with food as though it was their last meal. He knew that Jesus wanted his disciples to feed the hungry and give water to the thirsty. It felt good to be the hands and feet of Jesus. He was also grateful for handful of people in the congregation who faithfully served with him week after week. Much about the congregation frustrated him no end. Many people were not interested in change and were willing to do almost anything to maintain the status quo, even if it meant eventual death of the congregation. But each Wednesday he served with a handful of people who cared enough to arrive early in the morning, regardless of the weather, prepare a meal, serve it, and then clean up. He watched as some in the group engaged their guests in conversation. A few even prayed with some of them. Any one of them would provide dollars for food or whatever if the budget was not enough to cover the costs. There was much about Wednesday that fed his soul as the pastor.

On the other hand, he realized that other than what occurred on Wednesday, not much else was happening during the week to demonstrate the love of Jesus Christ to others or help the congregation make much of a positive impact on the community for the gospel. Also, the same six to eight people helped each week. No one else in the congregation ever got involved, even though they praised the work of those who showed up. Community leaders thanked him for feeding the poor, but he sensed that somehow these leaders wanted the congregation to be more involved in other forms of service. However, there was just no energy for people in the congregation to get involved in other community projects. When pressed to serve elsewhere, people always countered that Wednesday morning was evidence the congregation was doing its part. And even though Todd knew that feeding the poor was reward in and of itself, the ministry didn't seem to help the congregation grow or become more vital. Wednesday morning seemed like an isolated ministry island in a week of monotonous routine that was going nowhere.

INTRODUCTION

Missional congregations don't just do missional ministries. Missional congregations exist to do ministry to accomplish the mission. This means the congregation doesn't exist just to recruit disciples to act missionally when they are living life throughout the week, although hopefully that occurs. Missional congregations act corporately to carry out the mission. A congregation of eighty in a community of eight thousand understands that Jesus has called those eighty people to change the way the community of eight thousand thinks, functions, and behaves.

The emphasis on the individual in our nation has produced great benefit, both to individuals and to the nation. The downside of this emphasis is that the concept of community has suffered. Americans who observe the political landscape see leaders acting for their own political welfare at the expense of the community—unless there is an imminent threat to our nation's security. This same thinking permeates American Christianity and the church of Jesus Christ in our nation. We often preach and teach that mission is the responsibility of the individual, which of course it is, but in doing so we neglect the concept of mission for the community of believers. Often small, ineffective congregations are energized to act in concert only when their existence as a congregation, the status quo that produces comfort and security, or their facilities are in some way threatened. The rest of the time, mission is okay for individuals who want to be involved, while others in the congregation function as spectators living out their lives, using the ministries of the congregation for their personal needs when they fit their agenda.

The community of believers does not minister effectively to the community without vision and strategic thinking. Yet nothing energizes a congregation more than seeing God use them to bring systemic change to the community. Transformational pastors understand that it always begins with vision. However, without strategic planning and thinking a congregation may end up serving the community, but not in a concerted way that energizes the congregation and enables all of this energy to grow exponentially to change fundamental systems within the community at large.

Vision

I find that vision is one of the most difficult concepts for congregations to get, and for many pastors it is the hardest concept to articulate and then communicate regularly and effectively. When working with congregations, particularly smaller ones that have been in decline or on a plateau, I give them a vision to live out. The amazing thing is that many of these congregations resonate with this vision and find that it makes a difference in producing communal spirit, generating health and growth, and getting the congregation to focus on leading change in the community in which the congregation exists.

I tell the congregation that the vision has to be about two numbers. These numbers don't need to be in the vision, but they must be prominent in producing accountability for achieving the vision. As I've stated before, the use of numbers reveals the belief that we count what we value.

The first number represents the individuals who will become new disciples of Jesus Christ through the life of the congregation in the next five years. This in essence is the evangelism goal. If the mission of the congregation is to make disciples, the vision needs to be about how many. Such a number motivates the congregation and forces the leaders to strategize to achieve the vision. The vision itself produces change when the congregation realizes that business as usual won't work in achieving this part of the vision.

The second number represents the individuals the congregation will touch at least once with the love of Jesus Christ over the next five years. This includes people who attend a worship service only once a year, those who are fed through a food pantry, children reached in vacation Bible school who usually don't attend Sunday school, people to whom the youth minister on a mission trip, and so forth. The first number represents how the congregation becomes the heart of Jesus. The second number represents the congregation as the hands and feet of Jesus. The size of this second number is amazing, even for smaller congregations that have not made substantive changes and are not growing.

This second number of the vision is often the number that motivates people initially. Almost every American is frustrated with the personal inability to produce change for the better in the local culture. And most Americans want to belong to something or join with a group of people to accomplish things that are greater than they can achieve on their own. When a congregation can demonstrate that its influence is far bigger than the handful of people who are in attendance in the worship service, that congregation has much more leverage in attracting and keeping new people.

Such a number also resonates with younger generations who are often interested in being a part of group of people that is not self-serving but is willing to sacrifice its resources to help others.

The second number of the vision also plays well into the first number. God has provided a strategy for the church of Jesus Christ in the first two chapters of the book of Acts. Once the church was established, we are told that believers sold all they had and gave to the poor (no distinction is made between believing and unbelieving poor) as they had need. In other words, Christians practiced good deeds throughout the community in which they found themselves. We are then told that these believers found favor with people who were not yet believers. These believers were the recipients of good-will from those with whom they had done good deeds. Then the text tells us that the Lord added daily to the church. These good deeds brought the believers goodwill, which produced good disciples. In this strategy we see the two numbers coming together. The purpose of serving the community is not to make them disciples. The purpose of serving the community is to obey our Lord, which if done well produces goodwill for the church from the community. Then on the basis of this good relationship believers individually and corporately find ready recipients for the good news.

The church of Jesus Christ modeled this strategy throughout the first three hundred years of church history. In the second century of the church, the Christians were the only ones ministering to the non-Christians infected with communicable diseases during the major plagues that broke out through the Roman Empire. When the plagues were over, the people to whom the Christians had ministered flocked to the church and became new disciples of Jesus Christ. The result was an international church that had influence for Jesus Christ and his mission for his church.

WEDNESDAY MORNING: SIX MONTHS OF PREPARATION FOR WEDNESDAYS

The week being described in this book assumes the pastor has been in place between six and seven months. Consider what the pastor has been doing for the prior six months, so the pastor's Wednesday activities fit into a long-term strategy.

Before the pastor ever arrived, he or she was beginning to learn about the community through the Internet, visiting various websites, and other means. The most basic data are the demographics of the community, which can be easily obtained from the U.S. Census Bureau. Websites related to community government, the schools, all the nonprofits, and all the congregations in the community are useful sources of information. If distance is not a problem, the pastor and the pastor's family should have visited and driven through the community a number of times. Visiting on different days and at different times is a good idea.

While gathering this information, the pastor needs to keep a file of observations and learnings. Just like the pastor needs to make a note of the buildings and grounds the first time through, he or she should record initial impressions and observations that won't stand out once the pastor has been around a while.

Before the pastor begins to lead the congregation and if the pastor doesn't live far away, visits to farmers markets', flea markets, parades, fund-raising races, school athletic contests, and other civic events provide opportunities to talk to people. The pastor can ask them about their community, the things they like, and the things they would like to see changed. Every community is a microculture, and certain values, attitudes, and beliefs make this community different from the next town ten miles away. For example, often a rural town that is a county seat is very different from nearby communities.

Soon after arriving to lead a new congregation, most pastors get to know the people in the congregation. The pastor's agenda in meeting various individuals and families is much more than just getting acquainted. The pastor in a very friendly way encourages people to talk about themselves, their families, and the community. These individuals are likely to share their likes and dislikes and the things about the community that they find highly frustrating. Recently I was in a small town in rural America; its setting was typical of many small towns and picturesque. Yet many people in this community were frustrated with the local gangs made up of ten- to eleven-year-olds. Their frustrations were not only about the gangs but also about the age of the children in the gangs. I didn't have to speak at length with people to know what was occurring and that little, from their perspectives, was being done to address the problem.

Another element in getting acquainted with congregational members is finding those who have some connection with key community groups. Perhaps some individuals belong to the Rotary or the Chamber of Commerce, sit on the school board, are teachers in the schools, serve with the police or fire brigade, and so on. The pastor will want to cultivate these people to provide entrée, at some point, with the leaders connected to these organizations and community groups.

Also, during the first six months, the pastor needs to walk the community in those environments where it is appropriate. When walking, you can see a lot that you miss when driving. And on a walk, you get to know people, speak with them, and briefly interview them about the community, their lives, and what they like and dislike about living in the community.

The hope is that by the time the week described in this chapter occurs, the pastor has several lists. One could include attitudes, values, and behaviors that set the community apart from towns, suburbs, and counties surrounding it. The pastor should have a feel for the microculture in which the congregation exists. The better the pastor understands the community, the wiser the pastor will be in knowing the cultural barriers in the congregation that keep people out. The pastor will also have an idea of the cultural bridges needed to be built to help people find their way into the congregation.

Another list could include things in the community of which

many are proud. It may be sports teams, the school system, or the way the community responds to large and small crises. The next list could identify the problems and issues that people wish could be addressed. Again, this may be related to gangs, teens abusing drugs and alcohol, the school system, rundown homes, or junk in yards. A fourth list could name and prioritize the needs that the pastor thinks the congregation may be able to focus on. The pastor understands that certain problems may need to be attacked first to develop trust with community leaders and to build momentum before issues of major concern may be addressed.

Assuming the pastor has spent concentrated time each week focusing on the community, especially on Wednesday (following the format laid out in this book), the pastor should now have in mind a strategy to be implemented for the next five years to achieve a vision and see systemic change, not only in the congregation but also in the community. For example, in smaller communities the pastor now knows where people gather. When and where people gather demonstrate the institutions and behaviors they value and the issues about which they have a deep concern. In larger communities the pastor understands the key values and now has some idea of the key people in certain positions with whom relationships must be established to begin to move forward in developing and implementing strategies of service.

The last thing I'm assuming the pastor has been doing is praying over the community, much like Jesus prayed for Jerusalem when he stood on the Mount of Olives. It is helpful if the pastor can find a place or, if need be, several places where he or she can see the community or at least large segments of the community. Once a week the pastor goes to this place or places and prays for the community God is calling the congregation to change in order to help establish God's rule in that community. The pastor prays that God will provide wisdom for figuring out how to do this; that God will send people, either already within the congregation or new to the congregation, who will walk alongside the pastor and help implement this great task. The pastor prays that God will give the pastor the vision for what needs to be done, how that vision will be communicated constantly, and how the congregation will be mobilized in missional ways in order to see God work through its members to effectively lead change in the community.

Early Wednesday Morning

Again the pastor's day starts at 7:00 A.M. with breakfast with a community leader, a person on the pilgrimage of becoming a new disciple of Jesus Christ, or a leader (or future leader) in the congregation. The Scriptures show that God in the Old Testament and our Lord in the Gospels regarded eating and drinking as a key time for fellowship, remembrance, and connection. That is why such meal-times are crucial in the pastor's pursuit of making a difference in the lives of key people in the congregation or the community.

The second hour is again time for devotion. (The wise pastor prays through the day.) The pastor prays for the people with whom she or he will interact and for God to orchestrate all the situations of the day for ministry effectiveness. Today the pastor might spend special time praying for the vision of the congregation, the way God wants to use the congregation to reach the community, and how God can orchestrate events to lead the congregation to find favor with community leaders who might not yet be disciples of Jesus Christ.

Nine A.M. to Noon

The pastor today has three interviews to develop strategies and tactics in reaching the community. The first interview is with the principal of the local elementary school two blocks from the church's facilities. The purpose of the interview is to get to know the principal and find out how the congregation can serve those in the school.

One current factor in many communities today is the weak economy. Schools face severe financial cutbacks, which negatively affects their ability to deliver on the mandate to educate children and teenagers. The good news related to this phenomenon is that many schools across the country are open to networking with any agency, including congregations, which can assist them in their mission of education.

The pastor has learned that her or his primary role in interviews is to listen. The principal explains the particular situation at this school. The principal also wants to know what the congregation is interested in doing. The pastor is surprised when the principal pushes the pastor on the congregation's commitment. The pastor learns that other congregations have approached the school and developed initial ministries to aid students and teachers, only to withdrawal their efforts six to nine months down the road, when the congregations, for whatever reason, could not sustain what they started. Although the principal is hopeful that the situation with this congregation might be different, the principal is leery. In fact the principal says that if the congregation is going to get involved, it needs to start small in its efforts and slowly gain trust with the principal and teachers by demonstrating a sustained approach to help over a long period of time.

The pastor promises the principal that leaders within the congregation will explore how they might help and the long-term viability of their commitment. At the end of the interview the pastor asks if the principal would be open to a three-minute interview that would be recorded on a DVD. The principal agrees, so the pastor asks the principal to briefly describe the key stresses facing the principal and teachers in that school. The pastor explains that the DVD will be shared in a worship service with the congregation. This is a way of developing urgency in the congregation.

As I travel across the country, I have been amazed to observe that difficult economic times have opened doors for congregations to have well-developed ministries within the public schools. Congregations that do this well gain significant influence over individual students and their families, teachers, and administrators, while also having influence into how the school sometimes carries out its mission. The good news of hard economic times is an open door of ministry. However, I also hear stories that schools won't let congregations serve, even though there are great needs, because other congregations have failed to keep their commitments.

The second interview of the morning is with the town manager, and the pastor has prepared an agenda. First, the pastor is interested in the projections for the next five to ten years. Is the community going to grow, decline, or stay the same in terms of population? What are the business projections about new companies coming into the community or others leaving? What are the projections for the standard of living and other related information? All of this information pertains to challenges for congregational growth and for the nature of ministries the congregation may need to develop to serve the community well.

Second, the pastor wants to know about current and future stresses on the city in terms of safety, security, and the quality of life. Again, this information relates to the nature of ministry the congregation may need to pursue.

Third, the pastor is interested in the role that the city leaders perceive for nonprofits, including congregations, in dealing with social, economic, and culture problems. If possible, the pastor wants to learn how much help the city will give the congregation if it gets involved. Will congregational leaders have access to the information they need to serve well and to community resources that will enable the congregation to serve effectively?

The pastor asks the city manager for permission to conduct a brief interview and record it. Also the pastor asks the city manager to share the most current areas of need within the community. The pastor explains clearly how this material will and won't be used.

The last interview of the morning is with local Salvation Army officers. The pastor wants to find out who is ministering to local people without resources or power and how the ministry is being done. The pastor wants to discover how the congregation might be able to meet needs, either in doing ministry by themselves or networking with other agencies like the Salvation Army. The interview ends with the pastor recording an interview with the officers.

It wouldn't take a pastor long to get a real feel for the community if on each Wednesday (or whatever day of the week the pastor decides to use), he or she conducted a morning as I have described. Too often when it comes to getting involved in the community, it is ready, fire, and then aim. The more information one has, the more effectively one can strategize, and part of strategizing includes ways to mobilize and enlist the congregation. If the ministries of outreach to the community are the pastor's, they will only be as effective as that pastor's ability to lead and will end when that pastor leaves the congregation. That is why it is also important to interview members of the congregation about these areas before interviewing the professionals. Such interviews provide a very different and necessary perspective. Whatever happens in the congregation should occur as part of the overall mission, vision, and strategic endeavors of the congregation.

A SPECIAL LUNCH

Pastors leading transformational change benefit from discussing the process with pastors who have led systemic change and now experience the fruit of such behavior by leading healthy, growing kingdom congregations. Once a month, effective pastors should set up a lunch to interview other pastors near their congregations who are leading much larger outward-focused congregations. Often these engagements will be with pastors from other denominations.

During this lunch, pastors interview such leaders about leadership and all that goes with that large topic. These pastors seek to learn the disciplines that produce good leadership behaviors that galvanize followers to follow willingly, sacrificing their time, energy, gifts, and dollars to accomplish the mission and vision. They consider these lunches as leader mentoring, and paying for lunch is usually an inexpensive way of gaining knowledge and wisdom.

Pastors also use this time to learn how to be strategic in leading change. Leading a congregation that has been in decline or on a plateau to eventually make major changes is both an art and a science. Books, articles, and blogs can often teach the science. However, if these leadership practices are not implemented artfully, they can create such resistance that significant change usually does not occur.

There is another reason for a lunchtime interview. Often the larger effective congregations are reaching out and producing community change. Wise pastors want to learn how this is done and glean from the pastor of this highly effective congregation insight about the community and the key people to be contacted to widen a congregation's sphere of influence. The leader-pastor may be willing to network on behalf of the pastor seeking help in order to follow the model of the larger congregation.

Perhaps one of the most neglected resources for a pastor is the handful of pastors in the wider geographical area leading larger, effective, outward-focused congregations. The neglect may stem from several reasons. Such congregations may not be part of the pastor's denomination or theological orientation. There may be a sense of jealousy because the leader-pastor and congregation are doing well, while the other pastor and congregation are struggling to survive, let alone develop effective ministries to the community. In other cases the pastor may not see another pastor as a resource. Sometimes a local prophet does not have honor because she or he is local.

WEDNESDAY AFTERNOON

One-thirty P.M. to Three P.M.

Many smaller congregations that have yet to undergo systemic change have a carryover schedule from older-style Wednesday evening services. Often the pastor is asked to be involved in some kind of teaching during this time. If that is the case, the pastor needs to take advantage of this opportunity and continue to teach about the church of Jesus Christ, its purpose, and how that purpose is to be carried out in this culture ministering effectively to this generation.

The pastor would use this part of the afternoon to prepare for the evening session. This would be an excellent time to teach about how God is calling believers within congregations to reach out to communities.

When most people think of ministry, they have in mind the kinds of ministries that occur within the facilities of the congregation each week. For example, they think of teaching or preaching, serving by ushering or fulfilling administrative roles, helping in the preparation of meals, caring for the facilities, or child care related to the nursery or other children's ministries, or conducting ministry that takes special talents related to the arts or technology. Although these are valid ministry areas, they are limited in terms of a much broader view of the body of Christ. Just as there are a variety of gifts, the Bible tells us, there are varieties of ministries. Congregational members need to be challenged to think about developing ministries to people with physical needs, children in the school system, people facing social and economic problems, or people caught in the judicial systems or other arenas of life that create extreme stress and hardship.

Also, those attending regularly need to be reminded that their life experiences have created passions and concerns for different groups of people who are facing similar challenges. God may want these believers to move from concern and passion to action. That action may prompt behavior that enables a group in the congregation to reach out in fresh, new, and unique ways to serve such people.

The pastor has been gathering data about the community and its needs. This information will be the basis for developing a strategy, at some point in the future, that will mobilize many in the congregation to become involved in service. (For example, one-third of the congregation is used to fulfill basic ministry areas that help the congregation grow, while the rest of the congregation is challenged to serve in areas of ministry related to the community.) When the pastor unveils this strategy, people will get involved if the pastor has been preparing them in teaching situations, such as those provided on Wednesday evenings. Change does not occur overnight, but it does occur when a pastor has been eating the elephant one bite at a time. The pastor takes every opportunity to discuss the mission of the congregation and the vision, create urgency for the vision, or train for new strategies that will become part of the congregation's implementation of the mission and vision.

The last thing the pastor does on Wednesday before going home to be with the family is to make sure that the people who need to be contacted for Sunday have been notified or will be notified when they are present at the facilities on Wednesday evening. Wednesday is often the night when people involved in the music ministry and others rehearse for Sunday. It is often a good time to make sure that this time is used well for changes that need to be made to impact positively the dynamics of the Sunday worship service.

The Rest of Wednesday

The pastor spends the rest of the afternoon with the family, focusing the proper energies and time on meeting family needs. After the pastor's evening meal (unless a meal is served at the church), he or she returns to the church facilities to train, meet with people, and contact any persons who need information for the Sunday worship service.

A MAJOR WARNING

Developing a community-oriented ministry in smaller congregations that have been quite inward focused and, as a result, have been in decline or are on a plateau can be an invigorating and positive experience. In many cases it is the only breath of life such a congregation has had for a long time and provides a sense of openness to change and ministering outward. However, the pastor needs to be careful in handling such a ministry. If this ministry becomes another sacred cow that a handful of people oversee and protect, or if this ministry prompts people to say, "The congregation is not growing, but it does not matter since we are serving the community," such attitudes hinder growth and lead to eventual death. And if the congregation does not grow, the ministries to the community will cease when the congregation does. Several congregations in GHC have resisted growth but have opened their doors to serve the community. These community ministries are doing well (though not growing since there are not the people, energy, and financial resources to allow growth) but are demanding so much energy, time, and human resources from the congregation that the congregation itself cannot grow. The congregation and eventually a good ministry to the community will cease to exist because there is no growth in the congregation. Ministries to the community are important, but if they are not done properly and strategically, they don't cause congregations to grow and often eventually hasten their demise.

I find that congregations need to change if they are to grow. People who are used to having things their way at the expense of reaching lost people need to serve others by being willing to change. Many congregations don't go through systemic change because people with privilege, the Christians, are not willing to serve people who need Jesus, the non-Christians. These Christians don't want to be put in a powerless position. Yet these same Christians are willing to serve food to the hungry, give clothes to the poor, or work with uneducated, underprivileged children because that service allows them to remain in positions of power. When they serve in that way, they are still in control of when and how they serve. I believe Jesus Christ is looking for servants who are willing to serve from their positions of blessing (power) and from positions of inferiority (no power or control).

Both leaders and laity need to realize there are two kinds of ministries in a congregation. The first kind includes ministries that build the congregation. The growth of a congregation enables that congregation to have more and more resources, those resources being people, people's time, energy, wisdom, and money. The second kind includes ministries that cause congregations to give away those resources. These are often ministries to people in the community. The ministries that build congregations are like the accumulation of principal in a savings account. The more one has in a savings account, the more interest is generated. Ministries to the community are "interest ministries." If a congregation is spending more interest than it is generating principal, that congregation will eventually go broke and cease to exist. This is why when smaller congregations get too involved in community ministries without building the congregation, they are setting themselves up for the eventual death of the congregation and the ministries to the community of which many are so proud.

CONCLUSION

The wise pastor invests significant amounts of time in the first few months learning the community. God has called the pastor to lead the congregation to implement its mission and achieve the vision of changing the community by reaching many lost people and by redeeming systems within the community. Like a good missionary, the pastor learns the culture that surrounds the congregation in order to lead the congregation to function missionally.

Wednesday as Community Day is set aside primarily to learn about the community in which the congregation exists. The assumption is that each local community is a microculture that the pastor must understand so that a missional congregation can accomplish its mission locally. This won't happen if the pastor does not lead missionally by helping the congregation know both the needs of the community and the resources available to aid in accomplishing the mission. One of the best ways to do this is to interview community leaders.

A pastor's key resource in understanding the community is effective pastors leading healthy, growing congregations in the larger community. It is imperative that pastors connect with these congregational leaders to learn from them. It's important to network with other leaders in providing a kingdom effort to serve the community, and in order to accomplish the mission of each congregation.

I'm assuming the pastor has the opportunity for training people at some kind of congregational meeting on Wednesday night. If so, the pastor may use this time to help members of the congregation glimpse how the congregation might implement its mission and vision in the community.

WEDNESDAY

Early morning	Meet with a key person for breakfast. Use devotional time to pray for the community and the interviews.
9:00 A.M.-noon	Interview three community leaders, recording key responses in order to create urgency in the congregation.
Noon-1:30 P.M.	Interview an effective pastor in the larger community.
1:30-3:00 P.M.	Prepare for a teaching time in the evening.
Evening	After spending time with the family, conduct training at night. Confirm assignments for Sunday morning worship.

CHAPTER 7

THURSDAY: FINALIZATION DAY

Addison reread her completed sermon. She knew that it possessed clarity and order. The introduction was the proper length, the three points were logically developed, the illustrations were in the right place and provided understanding, the applications were appropriate for her congregation, and the conclusion helped wrap up everything well. But somehow, after all the work she put into the study for and the crafting of the sermon, she still felt emptiness in her spirit. Week after week, she exerted the same effort, and week after week, it was the same presentation. Yet the sermons, though done almost in textbook manner and communicated well, seemed not to connect with people or touch on the real problems and needs of living wisely and effectively.

Addison felt as though she had been given a recipe for communication. She followed the recipe accurately, put the ingredients together in the proper order with the proper amounts, and produced the same product on a weekly basis. Anyone could see the result was good and would please her seminary professors, but most of the congregation wouldn't and didn't use the product once they left church after the worship service each week. If she was honest, she knew she was often giving speeches that pleased the ear but generated no change of the heart.

As a pastor, Addison wanted to see her congregation experience the systemic changes that would cause this community of people to live missionally, both collectively and individually. She understood that preaching each week was a great tool to use in producing change. Yet she felt as though the tool she had, though used well, was inadequate for the task at hand. People were happy to listen and seemed interested in what she said. However, the spark that caused people to consider changing their beliefs, that produced new values and in turn produced radically changed behaviors, was not there. Although she understood that one or ten sermons don't in and of themselves lead to change, she was convinced that preaching that connected with real life and the real world was one of many tools the leader used to help the congregation move toward systemic change. That was not the case for her, however, because this particular tool simply was not working as it should.

Perhaps the greatest frustration was that she didn't know what to do about it. She was wise enough to understand that if something is not working, any attempt to do it better and with more effort does not work. She must approach the problem differently. Yet what was the different path that would lead her to be clear about what she said each Sunday in words that made sense and moved people? She was convinced that good pastors communicated God's mind each week in ways that caused listeners to know that God had spoken and that as a result change (whatever that change might be) was expected. She wanted the congregation to see her as someone who understood God well and also understood what it took and what it meant to live godly in a challenging world.

INTRODUCTION

Most preaching in our nation is bad. I say this as someone who works hard at the craft of preaching and has taught preaching at the bachelor's, master's, and doctoral levels. If I'm honest, I need to take some responsibility about the level of preaching in the country since I have taught others to preach. I do that right now.

I see two major problems related to preaching today. These two problem areas relate to mistakes I have made in teaching others to preach. The problems plague even pastors with better than average communication skills, who are disciplined, work hard at the craft of preaching each week, and assume the responsibility of not wanting to waste people's time in worship every week by being boring, irrelevant, or simply benign.

The first mistake relates to the amount of time between when the pastor studies the text of Scripture and other materials in preparation for the sermon and when the pastor develops and crafts the sermon for the weekend. Too often the time between these two segments of sermon development is too little; as a result, the pastor has poor insight into the text and into how the text speaks to real life (which impacts organization, illustrations, applications, and so on). My mistake was that I didn't demand this when I taught and didn't practice it during my first fifteen years of preaching. After I discovered that putting nine to ten days between studying for and then crafting the sermon increased my creativity one hundredfold, I never returned to my former way of preparing. This was and is especially true when I realized that such a process took no extra time in the week, whether I had two to three days between the two segments of study and then crafting the sermon nine to ten days later. I discovered that the old adage of "creativity being 90 percent perspiration and 10 percent inspiration" is true.

The second mistake made by many pastors is that they don't preach the way people listen. People live, learn life, and listen inductively. Most pastors preach deductively. That is, pastors usually share their main idea, topic, and thesis at the beginning of the sermon and then develop that idea as they preach. Pastors usually move from the general to specifics, but people listen and learn by hearing specifics and then move to the general truth or concept. This is the major reason why stories have been such a powerful means of communication from the time God created the world. Stories are God's favorite media in the Bible, and they were Jesus' favorite forms of communication while he was here on earth. Stories start with specifics and then move to communicating a general truth. They are inductive by the very nature of their structure.

My mistake was not realizing this for the first third of my formal preaching experience, and even after learning it, I compounded the mistake by teaching students to preach deductively before teaching them to preach inductively. Looking back, I recognize the logic of teaching pastors to communicate opposite from the way most people listen is quite foolish.

THE USE OF NARRATIVE IN PREACHING INDUCTIVELY

For much of history people have lived in cultures where books and other forms of print media were not available to the majority of the population. The average person was unable to read and write and therefore communicated primarily through speaking and listening. The easiest way to learn the history, values, and beliefs of their respective cultures was to listen to stories. Since stories basically communicate truth inductively, and that is the way people learn and listen best, people learned those things that were foundational to their culture. In such cultures the more someone could listen to and learn from stories, the more that individual knew, thereby making communal living valuable.

The invention of the printing press began to change not only the culture of the Western world but also many cultures throughout the world. The proliferation of books and printed media allowed thoughts and ideas to take up space instead of being only in the minds of people when communicated through stories, myths, and fables. Although deductive thought had always been part of the human experience, such thought began to move to the forefront in developing and explaining the beliefs, values, and ideas of many cultures. When one adds to this change in presenting ideas, the rise of scientific thought and the scientific method, the deductive communication of ideas eventually became the way to teach and communicate fundamental ideas, values, and beliefs in many cultures. This way of developing and communicating ideas was further enhanced with the mandate of formal schooling in many cultures. The result was that the inductive way of presenting ideas, particularly in narrative form, was often considered inferior to deductive reasoning and thought. (I wrote a sample sermon based on a narrative passage, using the essence of story as a way to develop a sermon, which can be found in the appendix of the book *The Art of Preaching Old Testament Narrative* by Steve Mathewson [Grand Rapids: Baker Academic, 2002].)

One example of this change is how the narrative portions of the Bible were and often continue to be handled in Christian colleges and seminaries. The narrative books of the Bible are portrayed much more as historical books than works of theology. For years illustrations (particularly stories) were viewed as vehicles to provide understanding and insight into theological constructs and truth more than actual ways of communicating those theological constructs.

In light of all of this, today the belief is that the best way to lead people and get them to change is to present them with well-reasoned arguments communicated in deductive form since that is the way truth is presented. Many pastors have said to me, "I keep telling the congregation what the Bible says, yet they don't act in repentance or change." Too many pastors tend to believe that if they speak the ideas of the Bible enough times and use enough scriptural passages for support, people will change because they are supposed to change. Although the Bible uses both deductive and inductive communication patterns, very few people are moved to change by reason and logic alone. After all, God didn't make us just rational individuals. God made us emotional beings who learn through our imagination and feelings as they are connected to past experiences and memories. The rational learners make up a very small proportion of people in any congregation. Further, when we come at truth from a deductive approach, we fail to take into account that God has made us to be people who listen and learn from an inductive perspective first. The old adage "experience is the best teacher" demonstrates that I learn inductively before I learn deductively.

The point is not to pit deductive and inductive presentations against each other. God made us to think and communicate both ways, and the Scriptures themselves use both patterns in communicating truth. Deductive presentation of truth has so dominated the preaching landscape for centuries that the average pastor with average communication skills usually finds little response to weekly presentations that don't take into account that speaking the way people listen might help in communication. Learning to communicate inductively coupled with the use of the creative cycle (putting nine to ten days between the study for and the crafting of the sermon) could really help the pastor use the preaching experience to lead the congregation to make changes God wants to see within the church.

Pastors with strong leadership gifts and talents are often good communicators, since God often seems to put leadership and communication gifts together. Many of these pastors prepare sermons and present them in deductive form. Such pastors can often get away with such behavior because their communication gifts and skills allow them to present truth using both patterns (deductive and inductive) in the same sermon, even though the overall process is deductive. However, most pastors in our nation don't possess either the leadership or the communication gifts or skills that allow them to communicate in this way. To use the preaching experience to communicate God's word effectively and see change, pastors need to think about how they can communicate in ways that encourage people to listen and engage both their hearts and their minds.

I believe pastors need to understand the essence of narrative and learn how to use that understanding to communicate well. First, these pastors will start communicating the way people listen. Second, everyone loves stories, which is why pastors have said for years they could preach the same sermon six months or a year later if they changed the illustrations. These pastors are saying that people listened only when pastors told stories. Third, when pastors take the essence of narrative and use it to develop sermons within the creative cycle concept, they will be far more creative and emotive and present what God has to say about how the needs of the congregation might be addressed.

The Essence of Narrative and Its Use in Preaching

The essence of narrative (story) is plot; plot makes a story a story. Plot is made up of three elements. The first element is *disequilibrium.* A person begins to tell a story, and interest is generated when conflict occurs. Usually the initial conflict is small, but then it grows in intensity. In many stories the conflict becomes so intense that it almost seems insurmountable. This is disequilibrium. In many stories the creation of conflict and its growing intensity take up most of the story. For example, in a mystery novel, the conflict is usually about who committed the crime. Often this is not revealed until near the end of the story. Disequilibrium creates tension in the mind of the reader or listener that causes the person to become engaged in the story. If the conflict is too slight, not well developed, or too intense, the person will stop receiving the story. As long as the conflict is developed well, the person is engaged and involved, wanting to know how the conflict will be resolved.

The second element of plot is *reversal.* The developing conflict or disequilibrium takes the story in a certain direction. The antagonist (often referred to as the villain or bad person) seems to be winning, and it appears that person's behaviors will win out. However, the protagonist (hero or good person) does something that changes the direction of the story. In essence the story reverses, and at some point in the story (often near the end) it becomes clear that the antagonist won't win. Again, in a mystery, the detective often finds a clue that begins to solve the mystery because the clue points toward the antagonist and the antagonist's actions.

The third element of plot is *resolution.* After the disequilibrium is resolved through the reversal, the storyteller deals with the implications and lessons. For years mysteries on television were designed to portray the concept that crime does not pay. Whether that concept was valid and true may be debatable, but the story had a point. I'm constantly amazed when I hear major Hollywood directors talk about their movies, regardless of whether the movie focuses on character development or action. They state that their movies, even those filled with action and special effects, were filmed to communicate a clear idea or concept through the telling of the story. Some writers and directors deliberately design their play, movie, or book to communicate several ideas, not just one. Even these artists design their works intentionally to help their audience realize that several meanings are intended. Resolution is fundamental to the telling of stories because stories are intended to communicate beliefs, values, and ideas that people believe are true.

Good inductive preaching uses the essence of narrative to communicate the way people listen. When one studies the text of Scripture and other materials in order to prepare a sermon, one studies inductively. The pastor looks at the Bible and other specific relevant data to see what is being said and then arrives at a conclusion. That conclusion is called a number of names; it may be the idea, the thesis, or the theme. However, the pastor has had the adventure of living with disequilibrium, not knowing the conclusion, and then through the exegetical process discovering what all the material really means. When the pastor starts the sermon with the thesis, idea, or theme, the pastor cheats the audience out of pursuing the same adventure. The pastor in essence starts with the reversal and then wonders why it is hard to generate interest in listeners. People pay attention to stories because the disequilibrium, by its very nature, creates tension. Tension causes people to listen and give heed to what is being said and experienced.

Once the pastor determines the main idea, the thesis, or the theme, the pastor understands that from an inductive perspective, the pastor has the reversal. The pastor's job then in crafting the sermon is to go back and determine how to create the disequilibrium for the audience so that the reversal makes sense.

A helpful metaphor is thinking of the sermon's main idea in terms of a doctor's diagnosis of a physical ailment. I hope the doctor has examined me inductively, looking at all kinds of specifics before making that diagnosis. Now because of my study and the conclusion at which I have arrived (the main idea), I know the direction of the sermon from a positive perspective. It is now my job to help the congregation feel the *dis-ease* for which this diagnosis fits.

If I'm given thirty minutes to preach, I avoid the main idea of the sermon for at least fifteen minutes or longer. My goal is to create disequilibrium with the congregation so they want to hear the diagnosis of the problem. I want to deal with the problems and issues of life and, much like peeling an onion layer by layer, move from the surface issues and problems to much more fundamental and crucial ones. For example, most Christians don't give to the church as Jesus and the writers of Scripture say we should. That is the first level (or layer) of need. The second level is that we don't give because there are needs for significance and status (either for us as individuals or for our family) that we believe money will buy for us. The next level or layer of problem is that we really believe that God cannot and probably will not help us obtain significance and status with friends and coworkers if we don't do it on our own. This thinking leads to the final level, which is that we don't give because we don't believe God and don't trust God to have our best interests at heart. After all, children of rich people, who know that their parents will give them whatever they want or need, are often very generous with their friends. They trust their parents to come through. Most Christians ultimately don't trust their heavenly Father to come through for them, in terms of what they think they need, so they hoard their money and attempt to provide for their needs.

If I can take people through the onion peelings, exploring various levels of thinking and beliefs that lead to certain actions, they listen for two reasons. First, I'm dealing with real life as the people in the congregation live it. Successful comedians (ones who keep the attention of their audience) describe real life in terms of specifics. Second, people listen because they are not sure where I'm going and how the dilemmas I'm raising will be resolved, particularly in thirty minutes. They wonder whether God has a reversal for their disequilibrium.

That is why I don't start preaching by turning to the text of Scripture. I often don't turn to the word of God until halfway through the sermon. Or if I do look at Scripture, it is to help create the disequilibrium. I want people to turn with me to the Bible because a thirst has been created for the need to live more godly lives, which means living in alignment with God's values. I want them to want to look at Scripture in order to find the reversal.

Showing people how to handle the issues raised in creation of disequilibrium develops the reversal. Most of the sermon after the presentation of the idea (the reversal) is application, and I find the best way to apply the reversal is to tell story after story after story. The stories bridge well how individuals have lived wisely or foolishly in interacting with the main idea.

The conclusion then becomes the resolution that drives home the main idea emotionally as much as intellectually. This is often a final story that puts together the main idea and shows how a person (usually not a pastor or missionary) put it all together and changed beliefs or behaved differently.

The Need for the Creative Cycle

Preaching inductively using the essence of story on a weekly basis demands that I employ the creative cycle. For several reasons, I need nine to ten days between the study of the text and the crafting of the sermon.

I need time to try out the main idea in my own experience, the experience of people in the congregation, and the experience of those who are not yet believers with whom I'm meeting on a consistent basis. I need to examine why my personal practices are often not in line with the main idea I'm going to preach. It is important for me to understand the *whys* behind my personal obedience or disobedience and those of many individuals within the congregation.

I need time to find the stories. As I interact with people, the message that I will be preaching in ten to fourteen days is in the back of my head, germinating—or at least the main idea is. Everyone I encounter and every situation is potentially a story that may relate to how individuals consciously or unconsciously are handling the truth I will be preaching. Also as I interact with other pastors and check out how other pastors may have handled the passage or topic I have chosen, I have time to examine their stories.

I need time to determine how I will unpeel the onion while I'm creating disequilibrium. Living life well or foolishly involves complex circumstances, competing ideas and values, and behaviors that often contradict one another. We all live with great inconsistencies, some of which we are aware and others we never notice. I want to get to the root issues in ways that are relevant to the congregation and make sense, and this takes time.

Finally, I need time to wrestle with how the passage or topic impacts the congregation's ability or inability to achieve the mission and vision. I want to preach not just to individuals but to the group. I want to challenge the group (all of us) to bigger and better things for God. I want us as a congregation to live wisely as a community of people and change the larger community in which we exist. I need time to determine how all this will be accomplished.

Developing Application

Once I have developed the sermon following the essence of story, I need to think it through as though I were preaching it. I need to envision in front of my desk a cross section of about twenty people from the congregation. I might envision several teens of different ages, college students or singles out of college, young married couples, people with grown children, some who have retired, single parents, grandparents raising grandchildren, and so on. If some of these categories are not yet in our congregation, I still imagine such people sitting there because if we expect certain people to show up, it is often amazing how God brings them eventually. I want to imagine their lives, their struggles and aspirations, their beliefs, values, and behaviors. I want my applications to be varied and real. I may not preach to everyone in the group each week, but I want to cover them all in a month.

I also need to imagine people in front of me who are not yet disciples of Jesus Christ. These people may be longtime members, occasional visitors, or people I have been talking to and gathering from the community. I need to think through how they will hear and respond to what I'm saying.

Finally, I need to envision the entire congregation as a community in front of me and think through how God can use the sermon to motivate this group to live out corporately an exciting and fulfilling mission and vision.

THURSDAY MORNING: SEVEN A.M. UNTIL LUNCH

This may be obvious by now, but start the day with a breakfast meeting that has purpose and significance. You then arrive at the office for your devotional time with God. Perhaps your prayers this morning might be about your sermon preparation and how God will use the sermon in the lives of people, not just on Sunday morning but during the week. You might want to pray for wisdom, insight, and the creativity that only the Holy Spirit can produce.

By the way if the schedule I'm suggesting in this book does not allow you enough time to handle e-mails, phone calls, and other communication, you might need to start at 6:00 or 6:30 A.M. Also, I'm assuming that as the pastor, you are working hard not to be out more than two nights a week, especially if you have children and teenagers living at home. That means that you must take advantage of the mornings. (I'm writing this as an owl who prefers being up late at night, not a lark who gets up with the birds.) It is a matter of stewardship and responsibility if you want to lead a congregation through eventual systemic change.

Once the pastor has finished devotions, it is time to work on the sermon for Sunday. The pastor focuses on the material that he or she studied and developed last week.

Using the creative cycle provided an unexpected benefit for me. Often as I studied for a sermon, I found some passages to be difficult to understand, or I could not see how to outline the passages. I was often amazed that many problems I encountered in my study were solvable as I went through what I had studied ten days earlier. I began to understand that my subconscious mind was working on this material even when I was not consciously thinking about it or the problems. I was able to state my main idea much more clearly and succinctly than I had on the day I did my original study.

Once I have my idea clearly stated in a way that is memorable and repeatable, I work on my purpose. Many pastors are clear about their idea but often unclear and ambiguous about their purpose in preaching that idea. I prefer to print out my idea in a large typeface and imagine it on a screen as people walk into church on Sunday morning. Assuming they can understand the words and construct behind my idea (it is not like reading much of Shakespeare), I want to ask three questions. These three questions are the functional questions I use in my study for sermons on Tuesdays.

The first functional question is, Does the congregation understand this concept? Does the idea demand explanation? Most ideas, no matter how clearly stated, require some explanation. Most ideas can be explained easily in five minutes or less. Many pastors spend most of their sermon explaining the text or passage, which is why most sermons are boring. Informational presentations are the hardest ones in which to create tension, unless the tension exists in the congregation before arriving for the worship service. If the pastor announces that the sermon will be an explanation of what the Bible has to say about sex, tension exists. If the pastor announces that the sermon will be about how the Bible validates "blue state" political agendas to a "red state" congregation, or vice versa, tension exists. However, most sermon topics don't create such tension, and if the pastor spends most of the sermon explaining ideas, she or he loses the attention of the audience rather quickly.

The second functional question that needs to be asked is, Does the audience believe this idea? Belief here must be understood in a biblical sense in that the idea is so believed that people act on it with some degree of regularity and consistency. Many Christians believe (in an intellectual sense) that they should give one-tenth or more of their money to the work of Jesus Christ, but most don't, thereby proving they don't believe that concept in a biblical sense. If the answer to this question is no, the congregation does not believe it, the pastor understands that much of the sermon must be persuasive, not explanatory. One false assumption of many pastors is that if an idea is explained well enough, people will believe it. The behaviors of most congregations prove that such an assumption is false. Getting people to believe an idea demands very different communication strategies than simply explaining the idea. It involves the will and the emotions because key decisions often begin there.

The third question is, If people understand this idea and believe it, how do they behave to demonstrate such understanding and belief? This question relates to the how-tos of preaching. Many people leave sermons wanting to do what is right before God, but they have not been given clear guidance on how to do it or what it looks like if they did obey.

These three questions determine the purpose of the sermon. In the study the previous Tuesday the pastor explored the passage, text, or topic upon which the sermon is based. The questions are now asked of the congregation, since how the congregation might answer determines the reason for which the pastor is preaching this sermon. Some sermons may answer one question primarily, other sermons may focus on two of the questions, while other sermons may devote nearly equal time to answering all three questions.

The goal of the pastor is to complete the sermon before going to lunch on Thursday. A pastor who needs more time may need to start earlier in the morning.

One other task to accomplish before leaving for lunch is to make sure that the entire worship service is planned and ready, as far as the planning fits the pastor's overall responsibility. Weekend worship services are still the front door for most of the new people who will become part of the congregation. This reason alone means that what happens during the worship experience is a major factor in the pastor's leading change. Again, if the pastor functions as the director and producer of the worship experience, he or she should handle details ahead of time.

Again, I'm assuming the pastor is to have lunch with a key individual who is part of the pastor's leadership development strategy or gathering plan of people who are not yet disciples of Jesus Christ.

THURSDAY AFTERNOON

Two major tasks are on the schedule for Thursday afternoon. The first task relates to visiting those in the congregation. I have not talked about visiting in terms of behaviors in describing the week. Medical emergencies and deaths don't conveniently happen so they can be handled on the same afternoon each week. However, as I said at the beginning of this weekly description, I'm providing a standard upon which pastors can base their behaviors in leading a congregation to eventually change systemically.

Most of the transformational pastors understood that they could not continue to be perceived as the primary person offering caregiving ministries to the congregation. Changes had to be made. In some cases these pastors were able to find a retired pastor in the area who could cover many of the care responsibilities related to this area of ministry. This solution is wonderful, but many pastors don't have the luxury of someone in their context or, in many cases, the financial resources to pay this person's expenses, let alone provide a stipend. Pastors who don't have an older pastor to assist them in care ministries need to develop a strategy to address this ministry area.

The primary strategy is never to do such ministry alone. By six months into a pastor's tenure, he or she should be able to recruit a group of people to go along on hospital calls, visits to widows and shut-ins, and so on. Individuals who have demonstrated they possess the proper gifts of compassion, mercy, and helps are candidates to be recruited for this ministry. The pastor provides on-the-job training during these visits. The pastor follows the mentoring model of having the recruits watch while the pastor provides ministry. Afterward, the pastor debriefs the individuals being trained. The pastor then goes with these individuals and watches them exercise their gifts and talents in serving others, and again the pastor debriefs them. The pastor begins to allow these individuals to go on their own, with times of debriefing to make sure that authentic care is being given. Eventually the pastor develops these people into a ministry team acknowledged by the congregation. The pastor at times casts vision in the worship service by having an individual on the team share how God used her or him to minister in a significant way in the life of someone being served through this care ministry. The pastor's aim is to set up this team as primary caregivers, even though the pastor knows that at this stage she or he will need to available for major crises.

The second major task on Thursday afternoon is to set aside three fifty-minute sessions for counseling or for meeting with people in the congregation for some special reason. Avoid more than three sessions a week. If people say they need counseling and your three sessions are filled, tell them you can see them next week or whenever there is an available session on Thursday afternoon. If you set them up late enough, which means you may not get home until between 6:00 and 7:00 P.M., people who work during the day can leave early and still see you.

It is very important that you set a policy with the congregation's board before you start the job. This policy is that you will see a person only once, twice, or three times for the same issue. If a person's issue cannot be addressed within three sessions, you will refer him or her to a Christian counselor in your community or in one nearby. Transformational pastors are not committed to counseling. If you as the pastor are committed to a lot of counseling, recognize that you probably will never lead a congregation through systemic change.

Train others to be teams who can help individuals align life more wisely and effectively. At one time such people were called peer counselors, but today's legal environment may encourage the use of other terms. For instance, people struggling with finances and debt issues can often be helped better by someone in the congregation who has experienced similar problems and has not only conquered the problems but also has a desire to help others. Perhaps one or two couples in the congregation who have solid marriages desire to help others struggling with marriage or even do much of premarriage counseling required by you or the congregation. Others may be excellent at grief counseling or helping people with life-threatening diseases. If the financial resources are available, you might develop a relationship with a local counselor who can provide training for individuals in the congregation seeking such ministries.

In their first years with a congregation, transformational pastors develop strategies to share the ministry. This is quite biblical as we see with Moses in Exodus 18 and with the teaching of the Apostle Paul in Ephesians 4. The tasks required for leading transformation won't be accomplished if the pastor or the congregation sees his or her role as that of caregiver and personal problem solver.

Of course, pastors cannot do all the training and develop all these people in their first year of ministry. During the first year, a realistic goal is to train one to three people to work with care ministries and one or two people to pick up areas of service that help people deal with problems and live life more wisely.

CONCLUSION

Good preaching speaks to people inductively since that is how people listen and learn. This is the way narratives are developed. Pastors who develop their sermons based on the narrative pattern, which is plot, can present their material in an inductive manner.

Inductive sermons begin by helping people feel the disequilibrium, which is the need addressed by the main idea or thesis. Once people understand the need and feel it, they are much more open to listening to what the Scripture says (the thesis or main idea). When this is done well, the pastor speaks to an audience ready to listen with anticipation about how to think, believe, or behave in light of the idea or thesis.

At this point the creative cycle works well with preaching in an inductive manner. The pastor examines the study material from the previous week and often finds that her or his intellectual understanding is enhanced because of the time elapsed between study and preparation. The pastor also realizes that usually there is an abundance of supportive material and application, which requires the selection of what will and what won't be part of the sermon itself. Also, the way the pastor will persuade is often much clearer as a result of employing the creative cycle.

Following the development of the sermon for the weekend, the pastor spends the rest of Thursday overseeing various care ministries.

THURSDAY	
Early morning	Enjoy breakfast with a key person. Have a devotional time with emphasis on asking God for help with the sermon.
9:00 A.M.-noon	Work on putting together Sunday's sermon.
Noon-1:30 P.M.	Have lunch with a key person.
1:00-5:30 P.M.	Deal with care issues and counseling appointments.

CHAPTER 8

FRIDAY: BOUNDARY DAY

Tessa found Fridays so frustrating. Friday was supposed to be her day off, yet she was never quite sure what a day off meant for her. First, as a second-career pastor who had a ten-year-old and two teenagers, she had motherly responsibilities to carry out every day. On Friday, those responsibilities were more intense, with cleaning, doing laundry, and often grocery shopping. Also, school events were often on Friday afternoon or evening. She was grateful she could attend, but it was her day off.

Second, her husband, an accountant, worked a regular nine-to five-week. Saturday and Sunday were his days off. There were times he could take Friday off to be with her, but never during tax season, and the days she wanted and needed for them to be together always seemed to be the days he had to work.

Perhaps the worst frustration was living in the parsonage next to the church. People assumed that if Tessa was home, it was all right to drop in for a visit and in some cases to seek her counsel and spiritual advice. She never knew how to handle these interruptions, particularly on Friday. As an extrovert and caring person, she felt bad when she sometimes pretended not to be home or rushed out the door on her way to a brand-new appointment she had just created for herself as a congregational member was coming up the walk. She liked people and she cared deeply for them, but as someone working hard to lead congregational transformation, she needed her day off to be her day off. It was bad enough that much of the day was already filled with errands and chores.

Setting boundaries in ministry is difficult since everyone in the congregation seems to have an idea of what the pastor's role is or at least should be. They approach the pastors with their agendas, whether the agendas fit the pastor's understanding of the pastor's role. Living in the goldfish bowl of a parsonage and responding to individuals in smaller congregations, especially when quite a few have bought into the image of pastors working only one day a week, make the establishment of boundaries even more difficult. Also, many pastors live with unrealistic expectations of who they should be and how they should act. Establishing and implementing boundaries in the context of unrealistic expectations may seem unspiritual and uncaring.

Tessa knew that she should have been clearer about setting boundaries and even more insistent in living within those boundaries. She lived with greater frustration with all she was expected to do as a pastor, mother, wife, counselor, caregiver, and preacher. It had gotten to the point that even when she had a day off, and she had little to do in terms of family responsibilities and no one came by the house, she almost could not rest because she expected someone to disturb the peace and quiet she desperately needed.

THE NATURE OF THIS CHAPTER

The other chapters on the days of the week follow a chronological pattern for structuring the day to accomplish certain tasks.

However, this chapter is developed differently. There are far too many variables in dealing with how a pastor takes a day off. One big variable is the pastor's family situation. Married male pastors probably approach their day off differently from married female pastors. Pastors with younger children handle this day quite differently from pastors with older children or those whose nest is empty. Older pastors, male or female, view their days off differently than younger pastors.

Another broad variable concerns recreation. Many people think in terms of strenuous activities, while others may want to spend the day pursuing activities that never get them away from their desk or out of their armchair. Money, location, and health are key variables.

I'm hopeful that the comments in this chapter will help pastors use their days off more effectively and efficiently in order to rest well for the strenuous task in front of them. The work of leading an established congregation through systemic transformation is probably the most difficult ministry task in our nation. The second is leading a new congregation (church plant) to grow quickly to a point that it is ready to reproduce and start another congregation. Most pastors/planters are not prepared for the work, stress, and conflict they will often face. What is even more tragic is that usually the spouse is not aware, and when the difficult times come, the spouse becomes frustrated, and emotionally and psychologically drained, leading to spiritual bankruptcy. The ability to continually recreate is crucial if health and growth are to occur. Unhealthy pastors and unhealthy spouses don't lead healthy congregations.

ESTABLISHING BOUNDARIES BEFORE YOU ARRIVE

The first agenda that any pastor establishes, whether in a call or an appointment system, is the conversation with the board or council about boundaries before becoming the pastor. The pastor shares that as the pastor, she or he will work hard; then the pastor provides an overview of what that means, with specific examples. The pastor makes plain the hours that will be put in and how those hours will be filled. Very few people know what pastors do, and as is often the case, when people don't know what a person does or see the person working, people assume the worst. When many pastors say they will work hard, most don't believe them. Previous pastors who provided poor examples of work ethic or results may exacerbate the problem. The assumption is that whatever these pastors were doing was not highly effective, which, sad to say, is often the case.

The first boundary that the pastor needs to set is the expectation that he or she will share which activities are being pursued and why. Once in place, the pastor needs to demonstrate that what he or she stated initially about work is actually happening. The pastor needs to be wise in sharing her or his work schedule at board or council meetings, but it needs to be done. The attitude with which these efforts are shared is not one of pride ("Look at all I do") or vindication ("I told you I would work"). The attitude needs to be that of a good steward reporting on how well the stewardship has been met. It is also important to share what is happening as a result of the efforts. A pastor can be busy caring for everyone in the congregation, but such effort, while making many individuals feel important and cared for, rarely creates growth. The pastor needs to report in the context of demonstrating strategies and tactics that will eventually lead to the future health and growth of the congregation.

The second boundary that the pastor needs to establish is related to the pastor's day off. The underlying assumption is that if the pastor works hard, he or she will be quite serious and intentional about any time off. The pastor will tell the council leaders what is expected from them in helping the pastor protect that day and how the pastor will deal with exceptions and those who don't understand the pastor's agenda. For example, anyone visiting the parsonage or the pastor's home on that day will be greeted by the pastor or the pastor's spouse at the door and nicely informed that the council or board has told the pastor to tell visitors to set up another time to visit or seek the pastor's help. A smaller congregation with no office assistance needs to place an emergency phone number in the church bulletin for the pastor's day off and also put that number on the congregation's office phone. This number needs to belong to a respected person in the congregation who is able to field those calls and determine emergencies from nonemergencies. The pastor takes calls from this person only on the pastor's day off. The pastor needs to establish examples before arriving on the scene to lead the congregation.

The pastor also needs to be clear about strategies and tactics. If the pastor uses breakfasts and lunches as work time, the board or council needs to understand that the pastor being seen in public places eating and drinking coffee is part of the job. If this point is not discussed before the pastor arrives and revisited with regularity once the pastor is in place, it will be misunderstood. This is particularly true in smaller rural communities. Pastors in smaller rural communities might remind leaders that the same farmers and ranchers who meet for coffee every morning, while enjoying each other's company, also end up discussing a lot of business in that setting.

Boundaries in other areas need to be established as well, relating to vacation, sick days, and so on. The pastor needs to enforce the boundaries until most people become used to them. It is better to relax boundaries later when people are familiar with them and the pastor has gained trust and respect as a leader. However, if they are ignored up front, there is no use discussing them with the church council or board.

THE PASTOR'S BOUNDARIES

If the pastor is going to ask the board or council to help establish boundaries with the congregation in relation to the pastor's day off, he or she must also establish boundaries. One advantage of being a pastor is that one is remunerated for one's time and yet there is little structure provided for how the pastor will use that time. Pastors usually are given an abundant amount of discretionary time to determine how they will fulfill their roles, and they must understand that this is a privilege not to be used lightly. Although it is great to be able to make dental or doctor's appointments at pretty much any time on any day of the week, that time needs to be made up on a workday or on one's day off. I'm not saying that the pastor should employ a legalistic formula; however, it is a stewardship issue.

It is one thing to stop by a supermarket to pick up groceries on the way home. It is another thing to be there during the day when one is supposed to be working. This is true in any arena of life. Many pastors today justify spending hours on the Internet or conducting social networking as part of their job. Sometimes research and social networking are part of ministry responsibilities; nevertheless, pastors must be people of integrity in their use of time. Character traits, good or bad, are often reflected more in the smaller aspects of life than in larger ones. The way that one handles time and expense accounts often says more about one's integrity or lack thereof than committing a major sin that may lead to removal from ministry.

An important comment related to integrity: reading others' sermons is a part of research for preaching; in some cases it is helpful to see how a particular passage of Scripture has been handled from an exegetical perspective. In other instances it is instructive to see how the pastor used applications, illustrations, or stories to communicate well to that pastor's audience. The integrity issue involves giving credit to the person who developed the material. Too many pastors have been asked to leave their current ministries because they preached others' sermons without giving appropriate credit. When I hear of these incidents, my questions are not about using someone else's sermon but about the pastor's work ethic and the pastor's integrity in providing recognition of others in the use of material. There is even greater authenticity when I take someone else's material and make it mine than in just using their ideas expressed in their words.

The last thing I want to say about boundaries relates to money. We as pastors need to model for our congregations what God expects of us in relation to our giving. If we are going to set a standard for the people we lead, we must live up to that standard. The same applies to the use of the rest of the money God gives us to live on and support our families and ourselves. I believe many pastors should be paid far more than they receive today. Having noted that, if I have made the choice to make my living from the gospel ministry, I must recognize that I will probably never be financially wealthy or even prosperous. I need to learn to live within my means regardless of what I'm paid and not begrudge those in my congregation who make much more than I do. It is my choice. As a good steward, I need to be sure that my family and I live within the financial boundaries of that choice.

It is important to set strong boundaries with the people in the congregation. I'm going to work hard, but I need time to recreate the way God wired me to do that. If I'm going to expect such behavior from the congregation, they need to see me, as their leader, establish boundaries within which I live in regard to my time, my money, and even my research for sermons.

RECREATING

Each pastor must find a form of true recreation. And just as the pastor is intentional about working, meeting deadlines, keeping appointments, and being disciplined, so too must he or she be about carving out recreation, which is required to be energized for the work. The work of leading systemic change or planting a new congregation demands the same kind of energy and focus required for starting a new business.

The temptation for some is not to recreate but to work without taking Sabbaths and times of rest. The temptation for others is to become so overwhelmed with tasks that they give up. Those who work hard need to understand that God has made us so we should follow prescribed life patterns or we will pay in full later. The nation of Israel failed to take Sabbaths for 490 years, so God let the nation be taken into captivity in order to give the land all the Sabbaths that had been missed. Those tempted to give up need to learn to eat the elephant one bite at a time. Declining congregations didn't get that way overnight, and they won't turn around instantly. But like any individual who seeks to live differently, for example, changing eating or exercising habits, it only happens over time. Perhaps the best reminder is to look at our Lord Jesus Christ, who near the end of his time on earth told his heavenly Father that he had finished the task. Not all had been healed, heard his sermons, or even become his followers. Yet Jesus meant that he had completed the course laid out for him. He had done what the Father required and didn't have to worry about the rest.

The pace of life is becoming faster and faster. The demands on us as adults, parents, spouses, and even children are more and more demanding. As a pastor, I must remember that my first allegiance is to Jesus Christ. As his child, I exercise my stewardship to serve well with wisdom and with fruitfulness. But as my Lord went away to rest, so must I, and there is nothing wrong with such rest, particularly when I have been fulfilling my stewardship well. I also need to understand that if I don't get a hold on the pace of life and change, it will get its hold on me.

I have come to learn that the excuse, "I don't have the time," is an invalid excuse. All of us have the same amount of time in a day. Anyone who is trying to accomplish something significant feels stress and pressure. Some things come easily for us, which may save us time in terms of our behaviors and activities; other things come to us with great difficulty. Working in my areas of difficulty or weakness usually takes more time. I must understand my situation and plan and work accordingly. I must also understand that I always have time for what I want to do. By understanding that, I realize that my use of time is related more to my priorities than my schedule. The better I know myself, understand the task required, and know and understand my God and God's expectations, the more I'm able to work wisely. Finding time to recreate is a wise choice.

God has ordained seasons for different times of life; there is a time for everything. The demands on me as a parent when my children were infants were far different than the demands on me when my children were teenagers. Today those demands are different yet again as my children are now adults and have their own children. I cannot have everything I want at one time, including certain seasons of life. I must take the seasons as they come and work and recreate accordingly.

Yet I cannot make the seasons of life an excuse. Living with infants is both joyous and frustrating. They bring the freedom of taking them with me at times, while at other times creating the sense of restraint as I'm bound to their needs and schedules. Wise people learn how to work around those times. I find myself quite frustrated with older people who use their age as an excuse not to serve God well. Daniel's commitment to his God in the lions' den as an eighty- to ninety-year-old was just as strong as his commitment as a teenager when he refused to eat the king's food or drink the king's wine.

There are times when the sufferings of life curtail many plans and activities. However, most of the time, if we plan well and wisely, God enables us to work hard in our stewardship and then recreate without a guilty conscience.

FAMILY LIFE

The issues related to time, family demands, and congregational expectations are far different today than when I started in the pastorate. I'm not sure they are better or worse, but they are different. I want to address two key issues.

The first issue, is that in many instances, the schedules of children are often as demanding as the schedules of their parents. Children today are often involved in a number of school activities along with other commitments related to lessons in the arts, athletics, or personal and skill development. On top of those commitments are meetings and activities for children within their congregation. These commitments often seem to intensify as the children become teenagers. The result can be a frenetic amount of activity for the children and their parents. As pastors and church leaders, we are aware that the average Christian considers regular attendance in worship to be one or two Sundays each month. Part of the reason that parents are not in church each week is that they are taking their children and teens to other involvements or using Sunday morning to rest.

I believe one modeling issue of pastors and their families is how they handle the pace of life for their children and teenagers. The temptation is to go to one of two extremes: allowing only church activities or helping their children do everything. I'm not convinced that either option is wise. I'm also convinced that I don't have the answers and am glad this is an issue now for my children and not for me. Nevertheless it is an issue that needs to be addressed by pastors leading transformation; they have busy schedules and must also wrestle with the schedules of their families and the families in their congregations.

The second issue is also related to the busyness of life: the issue of the family eating together. I'm often intrigued by how much the Bible has to say, more indirectly than directly, about meals, feasts, and people gathering to eat. The pattern in both the Old and the New Testaments seems to be that a key component of fellowship, connecting and living life together, is people sharing meals. I'm even more intrigued as I watch television dramas and reality shows promote the family, however a family is defined, eating at least one meal together each day.

The tragedy, at least from my perspective, is that the family meal table is often the backseat of an automobile as children, teens, and parents rush to various activities while eating fast food. Again, I believe a key modeling issue for the pastor is how the pastor and her or his family model family by the way they eat. Again, I don't know all the answers, but I do believe this is a significant matter. That is one reason why, in the week I have described, the pastor is home for dinner and is also home most nights.

If it is possible, the pastor and his or her spouse should plan at least two date nights a month. This will usually be on the pastor's day off but is not an absolute. As a couple, the pastor and his or her spouse should determine what works for both on date night. It does not have to be elaborate or expensive. It does need to be something that meets the needs of both spouses.

SMALLER CONGREGATIONS AND YOUNGER FAMILIES

A common situation I encounter in working with smaller congregations is that younger pastors are leading, since the congregations cannot afford to pay people with the income needs and expectations of a more mature pastor. Often these pastors have young children and are required to live in a parsonage since it helps the congregation financially. These pastors understand that on their day off, it is good not to be at home so they won't be bothered. Yet they often don't know where to go and seldom have a lot of money to do much if they do go out. I want to suggest inexpensive options for these families.

One option is nature reserves, which are often inexpensive to enter and usually are geared for families and their needs. It not only provides time together as a family but also can be used to train children to have a deeper and fuller understanding of God's creation.

Picnics are always an option. They don't have to be elaborate and can be held almost anywhere. Particularly in neighboring towns, local parks are good places to have picnics, as well as other recreational areas such as the beach, lakes, or rivers.

Local garden centers provide interesting options for children. Some have animals, including different kinds of birds and fish.

Many libraries are being updated to compete with some of the newer bookstore chains. Usually both places have child-friendly areas and programs.

Pastors might ask the grandparents or others to buy them a

family season pass to a nearby water or amusement park as a Christmas present. The family may go to the park on their day off through the entire season at little cost.

Good suggestions are available on the Web about where to visit and how to do it inexpensively. Like other issues we have talked about, having a family outing requires intentional thought and planning.

PARTNERSHIPS, NOT TEAM

The thinking behind a business partnership is quite different from the understanding of a team, whether the team is a business group or a sports entity. In a partnership the partners, while working together for a common goal, usually function with independence while supporting each other as much as possible. In a team each individual has her or his responsibility and continual reliance on others to fulfill their responsibilities so that each team member can be successful in fulfilling individual responsibilities. Married pastors need to approach ministry from a partnership, not a team, perspective.

One implication of this distinction is that the pastor shouldn't view the spouse as an unpaid adjunct helping the pastor fulfill pastoral and leadership responsibilities. I think the temptation to function this way happens more often when the pastor is male. In numerous cases I have seen the female spouse end up in a default mode being the unofficial congregational secretary, children's director, nursery coordinator, and so on. She so wants to help her husband succeed that she sacrifices herself and her responsibilities in order to be a good team member who picks up as much slack as possible. Soon both her husband and the congregation assume she will fulfill this responsibility.

The implication of being a partner is that the pastor recognizes the gifts and talents that God has given to his or her spouse. The pastor also recognizes that any piece of the ministry the spouse assumes is done not because of a team mind-set but because the spouse is fulfilling God's calling and helping the congregation fulfill a God-ordained mission and vision. The pastor and the congregation treat the spouse as special because the spouse is married to the pastor and yet is an equal in ministry fulfilling a key role.

One of our most successful transformation pastors, a male, has modeled this well in our network of congregations. When he and his wife went to a very small, highly dysfunctional congregation, there was a lot to do. At times his wife stepped in to serve in various positions as a committed individual in the congregation, not as the pastor's wife. They were partners in this sense, not team members. She now is developing a career outside the home while working on advanced degrees. On many days her husband, a very successful transformational pastor who works hard, picks up the children, fixes dinner, does laundry, and more. He sees his wife as a partner whose call of God on her life is just as valid as his calling. They have found a way to do all that it takes to lead transformation while being good parents and having two separate careers.

Also, this partnership enables them to be very clear about how they handle the pastor's day off, vacations, and other times they set aside for getting away from the hard work of leading transformation. In some cases it may mean one partner coming home from a vacation earlier than the other because of the demands of a current position and the associated responsibilities. In other situations it could mean switching days off so that the two partners can be together.

FRIENDSHIPS

Pastors frequently ask me about forming friendships with people in the congregation. Often the way that leaders and pastors answer this question depends on their experience with various congregations they have led. I'm convinced there is no right or wrong answer. However, key understandings underlie our behaviors in regard to forming these friendships.

If we as pastors don't like the people we are called to lead, we will probably not lead well. This does not mean that we will like a congregation immediately upon arrival, and we will probably encounter some people in the congregation we will never like. We may love these individuals as Christ tells us to love our enemies, but that does not mean we will necessarily like them. If we don't come to care for the sheep we are leading in order to have them join us on a very dangerous and exciting mission, we will probably not lead well.

We will come to like some individuals more than others. These relationships may be based on common family situations and shared likes and dislikes; these people may go out of their way to support us in all situations, but primarily in the difficult times, and they really are excited about the mission and vision. Out of this group most pastors and their spouses develop varying levels of friendships. The ultimate level—intimate friendships—is usually with those who are the most committed to all the changes that need to occur, rigorously support the pastor and the pastor's family, and have the ability to maintain the strictest confidences. These kinds of friends are rare. We may think we have such friends when at a key time, they reveal they cannot keep confidences. In my first pastorate more than forty years ago, I established a good friendship with someone, and the main reason we remain friends is the ability for both of us to keep the other's confidences.

The ability to keep confidences has to be tested over time. By that, I mean pastors need to share deepening levels of confidence over time to see how this person, who seems like a good friend, will keep those confidences. Many pastors go from one extreme to another, trusting without testing or never trusting at all. The bottom line is that if a pastor does not feel complete trust in any friendship, it is better to err on the side of caution.

I encourage pastors and spouses to develop friendships outside the congregation, where the sharing of information sensitive to congregational life is usually safe. We all need someone with whom we can share our struggles and hurts as well as our joys and victories. For pastors this may be another pastor in the denomination or in another community. The same may be true for the spouse. Be aware, too, that spouses may not always be comfortable with the friends of their spouses.

The pastor needs to find mentors and employ coaches. These are people with whom friendships may develop. They are also people who are interested in the pastor's ministry and understand the frustration and angst that often accompany ministry, particularly in transformational settings.

The pastor and the pastor's spouse need to recognize that the development of friendships can place them in a vulnerable position with the congregation, individually or collectively. That is why they need to exercise wisdom in forming friendships. They also need to exercise wisdom with whom they share sensitive information and how they share that information. Social networking, while a great help to some people in generating supporting relationships, is often far too public a place to share certain information. When more than three people know a secret, it is not a secret any longer.

By the way, good friends can be very helpful on days off. They can offer their home as a refuge if they are gone for the day. They may babysit on certain occasions. Also, they can protect the pastor and family from unwanted visits if they are the ones who field calls for the pastor on the pastor's day off.

SELF-LEARNING

Good leaders are always growing and learning in their areas of focus for their ministries and as persons. Part of the regimen on a day off is to set aside time for self-learning: reading, listening to or watching media, exploring the Internet, or pursuing other forms of self-growth. The pastor grows by reading and learning about leadership, healthy congregations, and better ways to communicate. These areas provide key development for the pastor as a transformational leader. Also, the pastor who wants to grow in other areas of interest, such as history, world affairs, or women's or men's issues, should set aside time for that during the day off.

Almost all the information one needs to know about leadership and healthy congregations is available in one form or another; it may be books, magazines, blogs, or seminars. Yet I encounter two problems as I work with pastors. First, many don't know the information. Second, most experience difficulty implementing the information, even if they know it. The first problem can be resolved much easier than the second since the second problem requires consultants, coaches, and mentors to help with the implementation. The first problem is resolved as the pastor makes a commitment to learn. Wise pastors read a minimum of three books a month related to leadership and congregational health. Growing Healthy Churches, which I have been asked to lead, has experienced a miracle in the number of established congregations that have gone through systemic change. That miracle has been assisted in part as many of our pastors have become avid self-learners, reading constantly, attending seminars and conferences, and taking advantage of other forms of learning. Self-learning is crucial for any pastor who desires to lead congregational transformation.

Recreation often happens as I focus on things I really like but don't get a lot of time for or as I focus on areas I want to know more about in order to grow. Recreation is not just about rest, sports, hobbies, and other interests. It is also about feeling better about who I am and what I'm becoming.

BEING IN THE COMMUNITY

Taking a day off allows the pastor to focus on something other than the ministry that is the pastor's primary responsibility most of the week. However, the pastor, as is true with any believer, does not get a day off from being a Christian and representing Jesus Christ. As the pastor and the family are involved in the community, the pastor needs to remember that although he or she may not be spending this day with many individuals within the congregation, the pastor may be spending it with people who may become a part of the congregation. The wise pastor interacts positively with wait staff in a restaurant, workers and others in the grocery store, and tellers at the bank.

A number of the pastors I interviewed printed special invitation cards that they and others in the congregation could use as they met and talked with people throughout the community. They used these cards and others for special upcoming events or sermon series as tools to start conversations that might lead to evangelistic encounters, invite people to a worship service, or at the very least let individuals know about the congregation and how God was working through the congregation to serve the community.

Sometimes as I was interviewing pastors or planters over a meal, they interrupted what I was doing to engage the wait person in a conversation about their congregation and/or other spiritual issues. Sometimes they prayed with a person or promised to pray as that individual shared about a personal need. All good transformational pastors and planters are gatherers. They are constantly gathering people, even on their day off. It is part of their lives and ministries.

CONCLUSION

Pastors should work hard; it is a part of our stewardship. I know of no congregations that have experienced systemic transformation or have been started as a plant that were effective without pastors putting in many long hours. Pastors not only work hard but also work wisely in order to see God take their efforts and grow their congregation by sending many new disciples for Jesus Christ.

Yet hardworking pastors need to take their recreation seriously. These pastors follow the pattern of their Creator and their Savior and rest. God has made us for work and rest, and both are important. Finding the right balance between the two is a spiritual matter that requires much wisdom.

Much of this book is about the work to which God calls us in leading God's church. This chapter is about rest and recreation. Rest comes after the work, as we see in Genesis. I want to work hard in order to be a good steward of what God has entrusted to me. I really enjoy my rest and recreation when I know I have worked hard to serve my God and my Savior, the Lord Jesus Christ.

CHAPTER 9

SATURDAY: ANTICIPATION DAY

Wren hated Saturdays. He never knew what he should be doing. Friday was his day off, but Saturday was a day off for most people in the congregation. Even his wife, who worked part-time outside the home, had the day off. His children were off from school. He was supposed to work, but what was he supposed to do? Most people didn't want visits from their pastor on Saturday, assuming they were even home. If someone was in the hospital, he could visit him or her, but it seemed as though many patients were discharged before the week end started. Wren admitted that he spent a lot of Saturdays finishing up his sermon. He didn't share that with most people, including other pastors. He had heard too many jokes about Saturday night specials. He was proud of the fact that if his sermon needed more work, at least he did it Saturday morning.

The other problem with Saturday was that even if he took it off, it was not really time off. He was always thinking about Sunday. He thought about the sermon, the worship service, who would and wouldn't show up, the people he would have to face who were not his favorites, and whether the entire day would go well or poorly. There were times he was envious of those in Seventh Day traditions. At least they worked on Saturday and could really enjoy Sunday as a day off.

Also, Wren wanted to see the congregation experience systemic change. He understood that demanded time and energy. He hated the thought of losing a day to the task of leading change. He recognized that most in the congregation were not thinking about Sunday unless they had something special to do. Yet if he was generating momentum for change, Saturdays seemed to slow everything down he was attempting. This feeling came about in large measure because he viewed Saturday as a wasted day in the week. Doing nothing was a poor use of his time, but knowing what to do that was profitable was really an enigma.

SIX THIRTY TO EIGHT THIRTY A.M.

In my book *Direct Hit,* which I wrote to help pastors and lay leaders prepare for systemic change, I talk about developing a prayer team trained to pray cosmically. This group is trained to pray for the big picture rather than for individual needs related to people in the congregation. In most congregations there is a group praying for individuals, but in many congregations there is no group praying for the congregational community as an entity and how that community will change the larger community in which the congregation is located.

Congregational health and growth are ultimately a spiritual issue, particularly if the primary growth is evangelism growth that comes because of the congregation's commitment to the Great Commission. Leading a congregation from an inward focus (meaning the primary congregational concern is how congregational needs will be met) to an outward focus (meaning that those that are not yet a part of the congregation get priority over those who attend regularly) is a spiritual issue. Such a change won't happen without the work of the spirit of God. In most cases such work is in response to the prayers of God's people.

Early Saturday morning, before the day begins for many people, is a good time to convene such a prayer team. Ideally this team meets every Saturday of the year with a few exceptions. By six months into a pastor's tenure, he or she should be able to recruit at least three to five people who will join him or her to pray every Saturday morning that they are in town.

This team needs to be trained to pray for a number of things, but first, the team must understand that this prayer meeting is not for those in the congregation who are sick, have lost their jobs, or have wayward teens. They need to know that other groups meet at other times for such prayer and those who attend regularly are being challenged to pray for these needs every day of the week.

This group needs to consistently pray that God will break the heart of the congregation, individually and collectively, so that the congregation might have a burden to see lost people in their community become new disciples of Jesus Christ. The prayer is that the congregation will have a "lost agenda" about its mission and vision. This group needs to pray that God will help the congregation focus more on those not yet disciples than on itself. These people need to pray that God will lift up an exciting, dynamic vision that motivates and energizes the congregation individually and collectively to want to see the entire community in which they live changed because of what God will do through this congregation.

The pastor is at the church facility at 6:30 A.M. to help volunteers prepare a continental breakfast for the group, who are asked to be there by 7:00 A.M. While the people eat from seven to seven thirty, the pastor trains them to pray and prepares them for the prayer time from seven thirty to eight thirty.

During the first few months that the group meets, the pastor uses the first half hour to train in what to pray for (an urgency for lost people, mission, vision, and systemic change in the congregation) and in how to pray (for the congregation as an entity to be faithful to our Lord's Great Commission). Once the people are oriented to the purpose and processes of the prayer group, the pastor can spend this half hour focusing more on specific needs. The pastor can share what he or she learned at the Chamber of Commerce meeting. The pastor needs to edit the comments to help the group focus on specific needs in the community. For example, if a new development is being planned within the community, prayers need to be offered for how God might want the church of Jesus Christ in the community to respond to all the needs represented in the lives of the families that will move into the development. The people might want to pray that God will give the congregation and other congregations wisdom in knowing how to evangelize the new people moving into the development.

During this half hour, the pastor can share what he or she learned from the interviews conducted in the community and the prayer needs that came out of those interviews. Also, the pastor might show edited video clips of the various interviews conducted during the week. The pastor leaves time for the group to generate prayer requests based on this new information since they will think of things the pastor has not considered.

The pastor can share bits and pieces of the interview with the pastor from a larger congregation in the community. Such a report then opens doors for the pastor to convey how this group can be involved in kingdom praying. By that I mean praying for other pastors and congregations in the community and how God is using and will use these congregations to help change the community. This is also a time to pray that God will somehow connect this congregation to other congregations in areas of service and evangelism.

During this time, the group needs to pray for one person in the congregation, and that person is the pastor. (The group is to keep in mind that prayers for the pastor's family or personal needs should be handled in another prayer venue.) The pastor needs prayer in knowing how to generate urgency for the vision in the congregation, how to cast vision, how to motivate and lead others to help implement the vision, how to lead positive systemic change, and how to be the person and leader whom God will use to help this congregation become obedient to fulfilling the Great Commission.

Other individuals need prayer during this time: the people who are not yet disciples of Jesus Christ but are meeting with the pastor. The pastor or members of the group may know of others in the congregation who are talking to unbelievers on a regular basis about their faith pilgrimage, and these people need prayer. This group needs to pray that the Holy Spirit will convict of sin, righteousness, and judgment and help many individuals exercise faith in Jesus Christ.

Obviously all these things cannot be covered in a half hour. That is why the pastor plans for each Saturday morning as part of her or his administrative tasks on Monday. There is enough variety that people can pray for a multitude of things over the course of a month and especially a year.

Next, the pastor plans for prayer exercises. Praying for one hour is a long time, especially for a very small group, which this will probably be for the first year or two. The group may use maps and pictures of the community to pinpoint needs. The pastor should break up the hour with different ways of praying for different aspects of the mission and vision, the community, the congregation, and evangelism strategies.

At various times of the year this prayer group might meet at different times or even different days to pray in the community itself. That might include prayer while walking various neighborhoods, going to the community farmers' market and praying for those selling and those buying, or joining other similar prayer groups in other congregations.

The purpose of this prayer group is to have some in the congregation asking God on a continual basis to use their congregation to be a significant instrument in God's hands to produce spiritual, social, economic, and civil changes in the community, beginning with the congregation itself and then moving outward. The pastor needs to be seen as the leader who mobilizes this group for this grand spiritual activity. It is part of the pastor's responsibility of being the spiritual leader of the congregation.

NINE TO ELEVEN A.M.

Congregations grow in proportion to the development of new groups and the development of leaders. Most pastors understand the need for groups, and often that is high on a pastor's agenda when he or she arrives at a new place. The development of leaders is often overlooked, however. Yet the development of leaders is crucial to congregational growth at any level. A fundamental issue that causes any congregation to bump up against any of the growth barriers is the lack of trained leaders. Almost all the transformational pastors I interviewed clearly articulated, in a variety of ways, the need to develop leaders.

Throughout this week, the pastor has been using breakfast and lunch times to meet with people who are not yet disciples of Jesus Christ or with leaders or potential leaders. Saturday morning is a good time to call these leaders together for group training, at least once a month. The pastor can provide training in a more formal, uninterrupted sense and develop relational connections among the leaders.

The primary focus of this training is the same primary focus we have been using with pastors in GHC for more than a decade. We train in leadership and congregational health. After all, the purpose of developing leaders is to eventually employ their gifts and talents in the development of the congregation in order to fulfill its mission and achieve its vision. Leaders need to understand this entity called the church, which they are being asked to lead.

During this time together, the pastor develops a theology of the church of Jesus Christ and the mission our Lord gave to the church. Also, the pastor develops a theology of leadership and how leadership in the church is like leadership in other arenas of life and how it is different.

A good pastor helps leaders assess how God has made them so they know where they are comfortable leading and what they are not supposed to be leading.

With this group the pastor not only develops the mission of the congregation and the vision but also demonstrates how key strategies, if implemented well, will enable the congregation to fulfill its mission and achieve its vision. The pastor shares what he or she is learning about the community and how God wants this congregation to grow, not for the sake of growth, but to develop spiritual human resources in order to see God's kingly reign permeate individuals and systems within the community.

This group, which the pastor selects by invitation, is likely to include individuals who are currently part of the formal structure of the congregation. More often than not, the majority of individuals will be ones the pastor has been recruiting and nurturing in individual discipleship during lunch and breakfast meetings. If such is the case, the pastor understands that part of his or her responsibility is to have a number of these leaders become part of the formal congregational structure. Then when the time comes for leading systemic change, the people making the decisions will be leaders whom God has led the pastor to develop.

This group will usually be small at the beginning of the pastor's tenure. After six or seven months, it might include only five to seven people. The pastor understands that within two years, this group needs to increase to at least twenty or more women and men (and some teens). The pastor explains to members that this is a special group, and that with the privilege of attending come responsibilities, which include reading books and listening to and watching CDs and DVDs; being regular in attendance; participating in field trips to visit other congregations or to observe different segments of the community culture; and interviewing similar leaders in other congregations or leaders within the community.

We live in a mobile society. Even in places throughout rural America, trained leaders often don't stay because of job changes and other events in their lives. Pastors need to understand that they are developing the kingdom of God, and when leaders they have invested in leave, they acknowledge that God is sovereign. They also need to remember that God can move leaders away and God can send leaders to congregations. That is why the development of leaders should be a regular part of the prayer team's prayers. The prayer team understands that the body of Christ has different members for different tasks. The prayer team's task is to pray for and follow their leaders. The leader's task is to lead while praying for the prayer team, along with others in the congregation.

ELEVEN A.M. TO TWELVE THIRTY P.M.

Once leadership training is completed for the day, the pastor moves into the office. The primary task for the pastor over the next hour to one and a half hours is making telephone calls. First, the pastor reconnects with visitors from the previous Sunday's worship service who have agreed to have lunch with the pastor after church tomorrow. The pastor confirms the details and uses the call as a reminder of the visitors' commitment the previous weekend or during the week. Obviously if the person is not home, the pastor leaves a voicemail or text message. (I will talk more about this event in the next chapter.)

Second, the pastor calls people who attend regularly most weeks. The pastor goes through the congregational directory and calls each person in turn. Depending on the size of the congregation, making these calls may take a month or two.

Before making the call, the pastor prays for this person and family. In some cases the prayer will be quite specific since the pastor is aware of situations affecting the person or people being called. In other cases the prayer may be more general since the pastor lacks information to know how to pray more specifically.

If the people are not home, the pastor leaves a message telling the person who picks up the voicemail that the pastor was thinking of them today and praying for them and that the pastor is looking forward to seeing them tomorrow in the worship service. The pastor also asks that if anything significant is happening in their lives, they should fill that out on the welcome card in worship as well as share personally with the pastor if they have an opportunity to speak.

If someone answers, the pastor provides the same message and then asks if there is any specific prayer request. If there is, the pastor affirms that it will be prayed for today, when the pastor hangs up, and for the next week.

This practice allows the pastor to connect with the congregation regularly while reminding people that they are welcome to attend the worship service on Sunday. In larger congregations this task can be shared among pastoral staff members.

TWELVE THIRTY TO THREE P.M.

The pastor goes home for an extended lunch with his or her spouse and family if they are at home. This may be the time to run errands with others, such as shopping for clothes, shoes, and so on. In any case, this is a downtime for the pastor on this day.

THREE TO FIVE THIRTY P.M.

After returning to the office at three o'clock, the pastor gets out the sermon that was completed on Thursday and spends devotional time letting the sermon speak to her or him. The pastor prays that God will first preach the sermon to the pastor before she or he preaches to the congregation. The pastor prays that the changes the pastor will be discussing will be taking place in the pastor's life now and as the pastor continues to act in accordance with the Holy Spirit's conviction about changes in beliefs, attitudes, and behaviors.

Following the devotional time, the pastor goes into the worship center, assuming no one is in the building, and goes to the platform.

For most pastors, everything about the preparation of the sermon has been in their heads to this point. Now the pastor preaches the sermon out loud to the congregation. I suggest preaching the sermon almost as though one were talking her or his way through it. A thirty-minute sermon delivered in this fashion may take forty-five to fifty minutes. While preaching this way, listen to oneself, paying attention to statements that make sense or are illogical; stories and their alignment with the points being made; and the transitions and whether they really bring people along. Transitions are often the most crucial part of oral communication since they help people catch up and review. They are even more crucial when preaching inductively. Also, the pastor listens to how emphases are made throughout the sermon. Sometimes the best way to emphasize a point is to speak slowly, while lowering the voice. However, if the pastor does this several times in a sermon, he or she also needs to emphasize other key areas by speaking more loudly and quickly. These oral techniques need practice.

Once the sermon has been preached out loud, the pastor literally walks through the worship service. This means walking up and down steps if the pastor is not always on the platform. It also means timing songs, announcements, videos, and other elements. If this has not been accomplished beforehand by others because the pastor is both the producer and the director, the pastor needs to do this and not just go through the service mentally. This rehearsal is critical. Otherwise, the worship service ends up being a run-through with its associated errors.

Next the pastor prays through the facility, asking God to use the facility as a key tool for what God wants to accomplish spiritually. The pastor lays hands on the platform, where the worship team or choir or both will be, and lays hands on the instruments the musicians will be using. As the pastor lays hands on these things, he or she prays for the people who will stand up front singing, playing, and speaking. The pastor prays that these individuals, like the pastor, will be used by God to do awesome things in the service tomorrow.

The pastor then works her or his way among the pews or chairs, asking God to bless in a special way people who will sit there tomorrow. The pastor prays for those who are helping new people connect to the congregation as the pastor reaches the back of the worship center where people will enter. The pastor continues into the nursery and Christian education facilities, praying again for those leading these ministries and for those being led. In other words the pastor prays for all the aspects of ministry from the time people drive onto the grounds until they get back into their automobiles and leave.

Following this time of prayer, the pastor goes back into the worship center to preach aloud the sermon a second time. The purpose of the first rehearsal was to listen orally and determine how the sermon sounded, how it would be said, where emphasis was needed, and how that emphasis would be addressed. The second rehearsal has another purpose.

Most, if not all, of us have had the experience of listening to a sermon and realizing at some point that we have been thinking about something else rather than paying attention to the speaker. This happens for two reasons. First, the speaker said something with which we don't agree. Our disagreement can be in any area of our experience, not just in regard to the Bible or theological understandings. Perhaps I felt the pastor had a different view from mine of how to relate to my spouse, how to parent, or how to believe about a social, economic, or political issue. Maybe I sensed that the pastor's statements offended others in the audience, and I wondered about how others might be feeling or what they might be thinking. As a result, my mind began to chase those thoughts, sometimes leading to other thoughts that had nothing to do with the primary concern, but as a result, I did not listen for several minutes. If the pastor tends to be boring I'm often glad for such lapses in listening; however if the pastor is interesting, I often wonder what I have missed. In the first verbal rehearsal the pastor thinks through potential areas that may cause the audience to lose attention.

Second, people sometimes stop listening because the pastor's statements do not fit logically or psychologically with other points or series of statements. If the sentences and/or paragraphs don't fit together, the minds of listeners try to make them fit, and as a result, they stop listening.

In this rehearsal the pastor works at making sure that the ideas presented fit together in a logical and psychological way. The test for a logically and psychologically coherent sermon is to preach it this second time with no notes, outlines, or manuscripts. Pastors use a wide variety of helps when they preach, and this is not to say the pastor should abandon these helps when he or she actually preaches. But the pastor should preach the sermon aloud at least once in rehearsal without these helps. Having trouble remembering what comes next in the sermon is often a good sign that the sermon is not coherent. If the pastor's mind cannot remember when there is little pressure (since the pastor is alone in a room with no listeners), the pastor probably has made some error in logic or in understanding how things need to be woven together, and that needs to be addressed.

One of the biggest errors I find in listening to many sermons is that the pastor just does not make sense, often presenting ideas or statements near the end of the sermon that contradict or negate thoughts presented near the beginning. Rehearsing the sermon at least once with nothing in hand while speaking is the pastor's best tool to determine how well the sermon and the ideas being presented fit together.

One more comment about taking extensive notes or a manuscript into the pulpit: television and other forms of media have removed barriers to communication. People sit in a studio, look into a camera, and speak to millions while making each individual watching assume the speaker is addressing him or her personally. Little children go on reality shows and stand in front of live audiences, plus all the television viewers. When given a microphone, they act like they have been speaking in such a setting for years. Therefore when pastors step onto a platform and need extensive helps to communicate, the listeners may have a hard time taking them seriously. This feeling about speakers is exaggerated when the speakers stand a long way from the people behind large pulpits. (In some traditions, where the pastor physically preaches is as absolute as the text of the Scriptures in the minds of many people in the congregation.) The more the pastor can do to make the preaching like a lively, interesting conversation between the pastor and the audience, the more it will be taken seriously by those listening.

The heart of all good preaching is persuasion. Jesus, the apostles, and the prophets of the Old Testament preached for a verdict. All of them wanted people to change. As good speakers, they understood that information, while fundamental to all change, does not in and of itself get people to change. That is why they told stories, reminded people of past experiences, mocked those who disagreed, and used other means to make their points. The Apostle Peter so moved the crowd at Pentecost that the people were pierced in their hearts and cried out to Peter and the apostles about what they should do.

Leading a congregation to successfully navigate systemic change is one of the most difficult tasks for any leader to undertake. In essence the leader is asking a group of people to embrace changing a culture that in many cases was at one time very effective in achieving a mission and vision and is often viewed by those in it that this is the way God wants them to act. Almost all the pastors I interviewed saw the preaching event as a key tool to use in achieving systemic transformation. They wanted the congregation to understand and then embrace God's thoughts about the purpose and nature of the church of Jesus Christ, evangelism, obedience (individually and collectively), and the transformation of the larger community through the congregational community. They also realized such change wouldn't come about simply through preaching, although they viewed preaching as one of the more important tools in leading change.

Pastors who wait to the last minute to prepare (which in some cases is a reality because of circumstances), don't rehearse, and don't pave the process in prayer are not wise in their use of the privilege God has given them. They are usually poor stewards of their own time and definitely poor stewards of the time of the people who come to listen week after week.

Another major benefit from rehearsing the sermon several times is that each time it is preached, the sermon becomes shorter, yet more coherent and understandable. I continue to be amazed that so many pastors preach more than thirty minutes, particularly pastors who are not really good communicators. The longer the sermon, the better communicator the pastor needs to be. Rehearsal helps any pastor work not only on the wording, logic, and psychological development of the sermon, but also on the time the actual sermon will require. I believe one major reason for long sermons is that they are not rehearsed, and the pastor is often saying things that need not be spoken but are because the sermon has not been worked through orally. Oral communication is fragile, and a pastor needs to make sure he or she says what needs to be said without adding verbal clutter or nonessential minor points or major ideas.

THE REST OF THE DAY

Many pastors I interviewed didn't want to do anything on Saturday night. Their desire was to be home and have a nice dinner with the family and a quiet evening. Some even said the congregation was told the pastor and her or his family wouldn't attend Saturday evening Christmas parties, picnics, or dinners being held by various groups in the congregation. They understood that Sunday was a key day for them and didn't want to lose energy and focus by being out on Saturday evening. Yet some pastors found interaction on Saturday evening socially refreshing and attended events to which the pastor and the pastor's family were invited.

CONCLUSION

Saturday is often a difficult day for pastors to know how to handle, but it is a key day that really cannot be wasted. The pastor needs to use this day to meet with the prayer team that prays for the mission and vision. It is also a day to conduct leadership training since often people are available.

The rest of the day that does not involve family time is to be spent in prayer and sermon rehearsal. The pastor prays for and contacts visitors the pastor is hoping to connect with on Sunday. The pastor also uses this time to pray for and connect with people who attend regularly.

The pastor rehearses the sermon twice in the worship center. The first time is to talk through the sermon to hear what has been written sounds like orally. The second time is to test the logical and psychological transitions and ensure that the congregation does not get lost in the presentation.

The pastor spends extended time with the family at lunch and in the evening. In essence the pastor really does very crucial work not only for the future, but also in preparation for Sunday.

SATURDAY

Early morning	Meet with the prayer team.
9:00-11:00 A.M.	Conduct leadership training.
11:00-12:30 P.M.	Pray for and contact visitors and regular attendees.
12:30-3:00 P.M.	Have an extended lunch with the family.
3:00-5:00 P.M.	Rehearse the sermon twice, and pray through the facility.
Evening	Spend time with the family.

CHAPTER 10

SUNDAY: CELEBRATION DAY

Aaron had ambivalent feelings about Sundays. On the one hand, each Sunday was exciting. He had the privilege on that day of standing in front of people and sharing from the word of God. The church facility, which was often quiet during the week, had adults, teens, and children making use of it. He was able to visit with people whom he usually didn't see in other contexts. And he knew that the majority came to have an encounter with the living Lord Jesus Christ.

On the other hand, each Sunday was frustrating. Aaron realized that often the feelings he had about the day were related to how well his sermon preparation had gone during the week. Although he wanted to see and interact with many people, there were a few he wished were attending other congregations, particularly if their attitudes and behaviors were not going to change. He was also frustrated by the empty pews, most of which were in the front of the worship center, symbolizing a small congregation on a plateau or perhaps in decline.

It was one thing to be excited on special days: Easter, Mother's Day, and Christmas. But when the weather was extremely hot or cold and one was going through the motions of another year, his sense of excitement was almost always absent.

He longed for the day when there would be a constant stream of visitors passing through the vestibule. He wanted the day to come when almost on every Sunday, someone became a new disciple of Jesus Christ. He would give almost everything to have most of the worship services alive and dynamic with the seats filled to overflowing. He wanted to know that people really valued his preaching rather than mouthing the perfunctory nice comments on the way out the door after the service. He had been in congregations that had all he dreamed and wished for, and he wanted all of that for this congregation. He knew that some of his dreams were to validate his ministry. But in his better moments he wished that this congregation would be one that Jesus Christ would be highly pleased with as part of his worldwide body.

Often, when the Sunday morning worship service was over, Aaron felt both relief and letdown. It never seemed to go as he planned it. He felt good about some pieces of the Sunday morning service, but he wished others happened differently. He knew he was his own worst critic. However, after years of ministry, there seemed to be little difference in the Sunday to Sunday routine. Yet Aaron was not willing to give in and follow the same procedures, week after week. There had to be a better way to do things.

EARLY MORNING

The pastor is at the office, assuming there is one in the church facility, by 7:00 A.M. The first thing the pastor does is to have a time of devotion. The pastor asks God to be the one who is honored as all the various ministries occur and as worship takes place in the formal setting of the Sunday morning service. The pastor also asks God to work through the pastor to accomplish changes that will be eternal. The New Testament tells us that when we proclaim God's word, we stand before people representing our God. We need to pray that we do so with excellence and great accuracy. It is helpful to pray through each aspect of the worship service. It is good to pray that God will bring the right people to worship and that the Holy Spirit will minister to those individuals through all that occurs. The pastor also prays that those who are not yet disciples of Jesus Christ will experience the Holy Spirit's work of conviction in relation to sin, righteousness, and judgment, and as a result, will become new disciples.

After the devotional time, the pastor finds a very private place in the church facility to rehearse the sermon one more time. This is the third rehearsal. This sermon has been marinating in the pastor's brain in one form or another since Thursday. Consciously and subconsciously, the pastor has had the sermon playing in his or her head since the two rehearsals on Saturday. Further changes have been happening, even if the pastor is not quite aware of all those changes. This third rehearsal is like a dress rehearsal. The pastor assumes that the congregation is present and it is time to deliver the sermon. I found that the time it took to preach the sermon in my last rehearsal was very close to the time I used in the worship service. In fact the time shortened each time I preached the sermon. A shorter sermon is not just a blessing to the audience; it is a blessing to those involved with child care.

My experience of employing the creative cycle in sermon preparation, developing the sermon using the essence of story, and going through three rehearsals prepared me well for Sunday morning. In most instances I could hardly wait to get up and preach. A highly respected seminary professor told my mentor, Haddon Robinson, that while I seldom hit home runs on Sunday, I usually hit doubles and triples. I remember Haddon saying he would gladly select any pastor who constantly hit for extra bases to be on his team.

The Need for Better Preaching

There are three reasons that pastors need to spend significant time on preaching and public communication. The first reason is that most preaching today is bad preaching. Bad preaching has a direct relationship to leadership. Followers must believe the leader is competent. And whether it is fair or not, many people consider the pastor's ability to communicate well on Sunday morning as a key element in pastoral competency. Pastors who don't communicate well begin behind the proverbial eight ball with congregational leaders since they are viewed as incompetent in a significant area.

The second reason is that good preaching is a stewardship issue. If the congregation averages one hundred in worship each week and the pastor preaches thirty minutes on average each week, the pastor is responsible for fifty people hours on a weekly basis. Boring people with the word of God, particularly because the pastor exerts too little effort, is poor stewardship of everyone's time. As a pastor, I stand before any congregation as God's representative bringing a message from God. Failing to work at this responsibility says that I really don't take this responsibility seriously.

Of course, there are times the Holy Spirit takes my sermon and me and does wondrous things for the congregation that I never planned or thought would happen. That is the sovereign work of God, but putting my trust in that work, week after week, while shirking my responsibilities is presumption, not faith. I also know from years of experience that the Holy Spirit is as present and active on Tuesdays, Thursdays, and Saturdays when I'm preparing and therefore does not have do the miraculous Sunday after Sunday because of the work I've done during the week.

The third reason good public communication is so important is that it leads change. Preaching allows the pastor to create urgency, cast vision, and articulate a biblical basis for values, the mission, and behaviors that align. The pastor can challenge the congregation collectively to follow the commission of Jesus Christ to go and make disciples. Good preaching complements good leading, and good leaders use the pulpit well in leading systemic change.

MIDMORNING

The pastor now meets with the prayer team that he or she met with on Saturday to pray for the community. During the meeting this morning, the pastor leads the team to pray through the facility, just as the pastor did alone yesterday. The pastor may share with the team upcoming events in the worship service that need special prayer (for instance, an interview on DVD with the mayor, a special call to giving, and so on). The pastor may also share the overall purpose of the sermon and how the pastor is hoping God will use the sermon to accomplish certain things. Then the team divides up throughout the facility and begins to pray. The pastor encourages every person to pray throughout the entire facility, even though individuals may start in various locations.

Anything with eternal value that occurs on Sunday happens because of the work of the Holy Spirit. Therefore it is crucial that the team be there early on Sunday morning to pray with fervency and expectation.

There is another reason for handling the prayer this way. Once people begin to show up at the church facility, the pastor must never go back into the office or be expected to be with a group to pray for the service. The leaders of the congregation need to know that the pastor has prayed fervently on Saturday and has been there early on Sunday to pray. The board or council should meet with the prayer team for prayer before the worship service.

A pastor leading a congregation through systemic change doesn't get to see most of the people on a regular basis, and the pastor needs to take advantage of the time people are there. Plus, as the overall director and producer of the day, the pastor needs to observe all that is happening in the parking lot, the vestibule, and the welcome and information center. The pastor can accomplish much in dealing with certain needs of people, greeting visitors, and overseeing the entire atmosphere if she or he is not in the office or in a prayer meeting. On this day all pastors are extroverts, regardless of their personal wiring.

Doing the Director's Work

By six months into a new pastorate, the pastor has trained all those participating in worship to be there early. This includes the technicians responsible for balancing sound and running any media. Since most of the people who show up early are there to serve, the pastor needs to meet with them and go through the worship service to make sure all know their roles and responsibilities. Actually walking the people through the service to give them a feel for what will occur is a good idea. At this time the pastor reminds people of the importance of Sunday morning, not only in terms of worshiping God but also in terms of helping the congregation, individually and collectively, become excited about God's mission and vision for this congregation.

I often hear from pastors in smaller congregations that certain people have the same responsibilities week after week, and they appear only when it suits them. I understand this phenomenon. If this behavior continues, it is a leadership problem with the pastor. Addressing this behavior may take longer than six months, but if this behavior continues into the second and third years, the pastor is not the leader and won't see systemic change. This is another area to take up with the board or council before the pastor leads the congregation. The pastor needs to have as much control as possible over how the Sunday morning worship services are conducted and who participates. In any case the pastor needs to have this preliminary meeting with those participating on Sunday morning before the majority of people begin to arrive, especially guests.

In many congregations adult Sunday school classes, along with some children's classes, meet before the worship service. If that is the case, the pastor shouldn't get involved in teaching or sitting in on classes. Again, the pastor needs to be freed up to be in the parking lot, at the front door, or in the worship center connecting with people who attend regularly and with visitors.

Welcoming Those New to the Congregation

The pastor's primary task before the start of the worship service on Sunday morning is to connect with visitors. As I stated before, many pastors who interacted with me said that for the first year, or even two, they were the primary assimilators of visitors and in many cases the complete assimilation system. These pastors understood the old adage: "you have only one chance to make a good first impression." These pastors were going to make a good first impression because they did it themselves until they could train the right people.

If by the end of the first six months the pastor is unhappy with the events of Sunday morning, the pastor takes the honest, straightforward approach. In welcoming guests, the pastor asks if they will remain after the service for a few short moments. In the meeting, the pastor does three things. First, the pastor lets the guests know that the worship service, though quite lacking, is a work in progress. Second, the pastor states that he or she would clearly understand a decision by these people not to return. Third, the pastor briefly shares the vision for the future and asks the guests to stay and help in achieving the vision. Interviewed pastors who did this said that visitors appreciated their honesty and often were excited about being a part of something new. Many visitors returned because of this forthright approach.

The next step to getting new people to join the mission and vision is to ask them to return next week so that the pastor and the pastor's spouse can take them to lunch after the service. Many people will accept the invitation. Once a consistent visitor flow has been established, the pastor on each Sunday morning invites first-time guests to lunch the next week and confirms a lunch appointment with those who attended last week and have come back, in part to keep the appointment.

By six months into the process, the pastor has trained one or two other individuals or couples to help carry out the luncheon strategy. Every Sunday one couple or individual follows the pastor around so that when the pastor gives the signal, the person knows what to do. As the pastor greets a second-time guest and confirms their lunch date after the service, this person interrupts, and the pastor introduces him or her to the guest. Then the trained member of the congregation states the understanding that this individual or couple is going to lunch with the pastor. When that is confirmed, this person invites the visitor to lunch the next week so they can get to know each other. Pastors have told me that usually guests agree unless they already have another engagement. The act of inviting people to lunch is carried on for as many weeks as the pastor has trained people, even up to five or six times.

There are two purposes behind this strategy. One is to get guests coming to the worship service on a regular basis. If guests come for three weeks in a row to keep a lunch date, they have already attended more that month than most people who attend regularly. And the pastor is probably having lunch with two to five guests at one time.

The second purpose is even more important. The pastor and the trained members of the congregation understand that there are several goals to accomplish at lunch. First, it is a time to meet and get to know the guests. Everyone likes to talk about himself or herself, so the pastor asks questions enabling guests to do that. Second, it is a time for the guests to get to know the pastor or the person who has invited them. Third, the pastor can fill in the people about the congregation, the mission and vision, and answer their questions. The last goal is the most important one. The pastor leads the conversation so that guests get to know each other. The more new people connect with other new people, the better.

If guests can make acquaintances with other new people the first few weeks they are in a congregation, they are more likely to make the congregation their church home. The main reason new people visit any congregation is to make friends. The best opportunity for making friends is with other people who are new to the congregation, and the luncheon strategy promotes this.

Obviously this strategy for connecting new people with new people has a financial cost. Let me suggest that this is another item the pastor needs to discuss with the council or board before arriving on the scene. A good starting point is to share with the congregational leaders that the least expensive mission field to reach and the easiest is the field where the people come to you. These are first-time guests. If the leaders are really interested in growth without a lot of changes they might find threatening, this strategy is worth the investment. If the leaders continue to be reluctant, the pastor might show them where the money might come from, in relation to other line items in the budget, and set a goal for how many new people will attend within a year's time to determine whether the investment is worth it. If that does not work, the luncheon might be at homes of people in the congregation or even at the church facility. Leaders will figure out a way to attack this problem, even if it means raising funds from people in the congregation who want to see change. The lunches don't have to be elaborate or take place at expensive restaurants. They do need to honor the guests who have taken the time to visit the congregation.

Welcoming visitors is the pastor's most important task before the worship service starts, after praying, rehearsing, and planning are completed. This is why the pastor needs to plan for those things during the week and finalize them early on Sunday morning.

THE WORSHIP SERVICE (BEFORE THE SERMON)

The gifts and talents of pastors and the needs reflected in a wide variety of worship services make it difficult to share what pastors ought to do each Sunday. If a pastor is a good worship leader and the congregation has no one to do it well, the pastor needs to lead worship until he or she can train others. If the pastor is a skilled musician and the congregation definitely needs the pastor's expertise, the pastor needs to sing or play until others are trained. Each congregation is different, as are the talents of the pastor. The bottom line is that the pastor must make the Sunday morning experience as good as it can possibly be, even though it may be far from where it needs to be and will be for several years. In most small congregations that are in decline or on a plateau, the worship service is still the doorway most new people enter to become part of the congregation.

The pastor is personally responsible for certain things, and he or she must make sure they happen. As already stated, the pastor must become the producer and director of the service. Since this venue is so crucial to the life of the congregation, these responsibilities cannot be delegated. I find that in many large congregations the pastor is still the ultimate producer and director, even though the pastor might work through others and delegate much of what happens in the various arenas related to the entire service. If larger congregational pastors understand this, it really must be true for smaller congregations.

The pastor is quite clear that he or she should know what every person is going to say while in front of the congregation. In missional congregations, guests are treated as guests. That is, the service is not tailored for what we might think guests want to happen, but there is a consistent attempt to make worship understandable so that guests won't feel awkward or stand out in any way that might embarrass them. There are always clear explanations for any behaviors required of the congregation, such as observing the Lord's Table, kneeling, greeting one another, and so on. It also means that language does not offend. It is one thing if the truth of the gospel offends someone. It is an entirely different matter if we offend people because we have not thought through what we are going to say. For example, no one should speak or pray in King James-like English since most people today don't talk that way. We must be careful not to say, even in a joking manner, things that offend people with whom we don't agree. And we need to avoid insider terms that people with little or no church background don't understand. This is why the pastor as director needs to have people rehearse and understand their roles when standing in front of the congregation and speaking.

The pastor makes sure that he or she welcomes guests and asks them for information. Until someone can be trained to do this, as the pastor would, this is not delegated, especially in smaller congregations where people need to connect with the pastor. This welcome must feel fresh and new each week, even if it is the same. Perfunctory welcomes inspire no guest to do what is asked or in some cases return for a second visit.

If the pastor has planned an element in the service to either create urgency or cast vision, he or she needs to be involved. Creating urgency and casting vision are the pastor's responsibilities, and the pastor assures that these elements are carried out with excellence.

The pastor needs to oversee special events, such as infant baptisms, baby dedications, baptisms, introduction of new disciples, and welcome of new members, especially in smaller congregations. There are two reasons. First, the pastor provides leadership oversight of the body collectively while honoring individuals. Second, these events are ideal situations for casting vision. For example, honoring children through baptism or dedication allows the pastor to talk about the future and how the congregation one day is going to minister effectively to far more children, both within the walls of the church and within the community.

The pastor should always receive the offering, which is a vital act of worship. The pastor needs to use the brief time allotted to tell a story of how God uses finances to produce spiritual dividends. A strong congregation with which I consulted had an excellent track record in giving. The reason was that every Sunday the pastor provided a story from current or biblical times to relate money to ministry. The people understood that giving was not an obligation to be carried out grudgingly but an opportunity to share financially in ministries that changed lives for all eternity. This congregation had this sound understanding because of the pastor's commitment to use that time well Sunday after Sunday.

THE SERMON

Preaching today is increasingly difficult because of people's exposure to media outside the life of the congregation. There was a day in the past when debates, speeches, and monologues were a basic form of entertainment for most people. However, those days are long gone. The pastor each week is competing with a media-saturated congregation accustomed to visual interaction that includes color, fast-paced change, and multiple messages occurring at the same time, accompanied by sound and music that reach us at a visceral level. People today typically don't listen to extended monologues designed to move individuals and groups to decisions unless they are forced to do so. The nation may listen to a presidential speech after a major crisis because of fear and anger, but without extreme circumstances surrounding the reason for the president to speak, few listen and pay attention. Pastors today work against mounting cultural odds.

Every commercial on television attempts to persuade us about an idea. Good pastors understand that persuasion causes people to listen. It is not information unless people desperately feel they need information to better their lives. And the sponsor's product will help us make that idea a reality in our lives. I may use information (the word of God) to help people feel a need, meet a need, or live well in regard to the demands of life, but ultimately a pastor attempts to persuade people to think and act in a proper way in relation to the information being presented. This is another reason for preaching inductively as opposed to deductively. All good persuasive arguments are developed inductively since the speaker realizes that the audience is hostile to the idea. The bottom line each Sunday is for the pastor to persuade. If the pastor takes such a stance, he or she will automatically increase the ability to communicate better with an audience.

The pastor also needs to understand that oral communication is fragile and that many things can distract listeners from giving the pastor their attention. Pastors require as few physical barriers as possible between them and the congregation. Pulpits, large displays of flowers, railings, and great distances are hindrances to the communication process. Pastors leading change realize that these barriers need to eventually be eliminated. Often it takes more than six months to remove physical barriers that have taken on absolute standing, much like the table of showbread in the Old Testament temple. If these barriers are not addressed at some point, they will continue to hinder reaching people and communicating well to a generation used to new communication tools being released every few months.

Pastors today are keenly aware of their wording. If the congregation is growing because people from the community are attending, the pastor understands that these new guests have a limited understanding of insider "church" terminology and won't tolerate unguarded language about groups, ideas, and people they may see as their cultural heroes. The pastor also makes sure that people without Bibles are given them and then are helped in finding their way around this book that may be quite unfamiliar to them.

The bottom line is that the pastor as producer and director of worship is as committed to having the sermon go well in terms of the overall worship experience as the rest of the elements in Sunday morning worship.

LUNCH MEETING AFTER THE WORSHIP SERVICE

After the worship service, the pastor interacts with those who have attended that day. The pastor may want to connect with key leaders or people the pastor will be meeting with during the week, or other individuals with whom it is important to touch base. However, this time of interaction should be somewhat limited in light of the guests the pastor is planning to meet for lunch.

If the pastor has no guests and the past or next week is such that the pastor or others cannot meet, the time after the worship service is an opportunity to do leadership training. In our fast-paced culture it is sometimes easier for people to stay after the worship service than return at another time or set up another appointment during the week. Such meetings might involve food that all have prepared so the pastor can eat with these individuals and then get right into training around the table.

When the pastor goes to lunch with several guests, who visited for the first time last week, the pastor has a specific agenda for the meeting. First, the pastor wants to get to know the guests. The pastor is not just interested in finding out about who these people are, what they have done, and what their interests are. The pastor also attempts to find out to some degree where these individuals are in their spiritual pilgrimages with God. With the information about their spiritual pilgrimages, the pastor knows how to pray and develop a strategy for interacting with these individuals to help them grow as disciples or become new disciples of Jesus Christ.

Second, the pastor wants to help these individuals learn about the pastor and the pastor's family. The pastor is always recruiting people to Jesus Christ first and to the mission and vision of the congregation second. All good recruitment is based on relationships; the better the relationship between the pastor and the guests, the easier it is to recruit.

Third, the pastor goes through his or her stump speech that articulates the mission and vision of the congregation. The pastor tailors the speech to the dreams and experiences learned from the guests as they have shared. The pastor's desire is to match as much as possible the dreams and visions of the guests to the mission and vision of the congregation.

Fourth, the pastor works hard at developing relationships between the guests. The pastor wants these individuals to learn about each other and to find common ground that will cause them to want to connect past this lunch. People who make new friends in the congregation often stay because of those friendships. New people are generally not going to make friends with those who have been attending regularly for a number of years. Those who have been attending for a while have all the friends they can handle, and they find it difficult to make new friends. If new people are going to make friends, the friendships should be with others new to the congregation.

Some people who have left a congregation in the past may consider returning since a new pastor is in place. As the new pastor meets with these individuals, he or she should be highly skeptical. In some cases these are good people who were treated poorly by some individuals in the congregation, which caused them to leave. A former pastor, the board or council, or another key individual in the congregation may have been involved. But in the majority of cases the people themselves were the problem. Whatever story they tell the new pastor may be true from their perspective, but others may view it quite differently. Sometimes a former pastor might have done the congregation and the new pastor a favor by helping these people leave. It is always good to get all the facts, including talking to former pastors if that is possible. Even having the facts, the pastor should provide a way for these individuals to prove themselves before placing them in key positions of leadership.

Some congregations experience growth because of problems in neighboring congregations. Most pastors have come to realize that no matter how small their congregations might be and no matter how much they want to see growth, most of the time they don't want people who have left other congregations. Most of our pastors in GHC have fairly frank conversations with such people when they meet with them for the first time. They ask about why the people are leaving, so the pastors get at least one side of the story. They tell the people that they will call the pastor of the congregation these people are leaving to find out that pastor's perspective. They also let them know that if they discover they left their former congregation making many complaints to whomever would listen (individually and collectively, even for good reasons), they won't be welcome in this congregation.

In smaller congregations any growth is usually highly prized, but wise pastors realize that not all growth is good growth. Also, missional pastors know that the best growth is conversion growth. A healthy congregation grows through the process of reproduction.

SUNDAY AFTERNOON

Back at home on Sunday afternoon, the pastor makes one-minute phone calls to people who visited for the first time that morning. Whether you get them or just leave a message, thank them for coming, invite them again to lunch next Sunday, let them know how to RSVP if they have not already done so, and state that you would be happy to meet with them at another time if next Sunday does not work. If you get them on the phone, don't talk long, even though you sense they feel some obligation to have a conversation with you. Communicate that you care, but you are not going to verbally stalk them until they return or never come back. One pastor, an avid pro football fan, said he made the calls during commercials, which forced him to be brief.

The next task is to call or e-mail leaders and others to respond to things you learned during the morning or to set up or confirm meetings and appointments for the next week.

This is good time to rehearse the events of the morning, including the worship service, while it is fresh. Make notes about what went well, what requires improvement, or what could at least be done better. Think through whom you need to spend time with and how you will approach them about changes. Send congratulatory e-mails or leave voicemails to honor those who did things well and helped the morning be a success.

If you can handle it emotionally—some pastors may have to wait a day or two—watch your sermon. All good pastors are constantly working at getting better, and part of that is watching yourself, no matter how painful that might be. Most good pastors are made, not born; they have to constantly work at their craft in order to improve. Great preaching relates to one's gift. However, many pastors who communicate poorly can become good if they work at the craft.

If you have trained your leaders well, they have already e-mailed attendance figures and giving amounts to you. This information allows you to determine what is happening and see where the congregation is compared to the same Sunday a year ago.

Some of you reading this might remember we talked about doing some of these tasks on Monday. The more you can get done on Sunday afternoon, the more discretionary time you will have during the week to complete other tasks.

Having said that, I wouldn't work on these tasks (except the one-minute phone calls) past 4:00 P.M. on Sunday. I also would not work on them if I have responsibilities Sunday night. Sundays are draining physically, emotionally, and spiritually. The pastor has been involved in spiritual work and in the process has used up large amounts of adrenaline. If you are doing any ministry Sunday evening, you will probably need to rest Sunday afternoon.

LATE AFTERNOON AND EVENING

My preference was not to do anything late Sunday afternoon and evening. It was the best time of the week for me in terms of rest and relaxation; it was even better than my day off. The week was over, and if I worked hard, I could relax completely, knowing that I had been a good steward before God with all that God had given me to do. It was the time of the week that had the least pressure. It was time to enjoy my family and completely do what my spouse and I wanted to do, even if it was nothing.

CONCLUSION

If you have just completed reading, not skimming, this book, you are probably exhausted. I understand that feeling since I have just finished writing it. Part of me hopes this book has exhausted you. Leading congregational transformation or planting a highly effective new congregation is not for the fainthearted. These tasks require women and men of God who have passion for the church of Jesus Christ and its mission to make more and more new disciples for Jesus Christ. It requires courage, stamina, tenacity, learning, and great wisdom. Leading transformation or planting new congregations are our responsibilities. God's responsibility is to take what we have done and grow the church, which God has promised to do.

If this book has scared you away from leading congregational transformation, that result is also a good one from my perspective. There is nothing more frustrating than attempting a task that you don't understand, are not wired to do, and are not cut out for in terms of your physical and spiritual DNA. If that is the case for you, I encourage you to consider doing something else than being a pastor. If a congregation that is on a plateau, in decline, or not growing by consistently making new disciples is living in disobedience, your role as a leader of such a congregation needs to be questioned. Now if you believe that the assumptions I have made about the church of Jesus Christ and its local congregations are incorrect, the choice for you is a different one. But if you agree that what I have been saying is valid, you should try to do what it takes to lead such change.

Leading such change is not easy for the most gifted leaders. It is much harder for people who struggle to lead in ways that come naturally for more gifted persons. However, I want to honor you who join the battle and take risks, even though you may not be as gifted as some others. You are the true heroes of the faith in our nation. I find great delight in consulting with smaller, disobedient congregations that are led by pastors who are not as gifted as all the famous ones we hear about, and helping that pastor and that pastor's congregation see God bless with health and growth as that congregation becomes obedient to Jesus Christ. We have seen that happen again and again in GHC throughout the United States, Canada, Australia, and New Zealand. You are the women and men of faith who would have their names in Hebrews 11 if that book were to be written today.

The task is a difficult one that takes courage and hard work, but the mission to which our Lord calls us is not impossible. He will build his church. He also works through the women and men who serve as good stewards and want to obey his command to go and make disciples.

SUNDAY

Early morning	Have a devotional time Rehearse sermon.
Midmorning	Pray with prayer team. Do the director's work with participants in the worship service. Greet new people. Extend care to those who attend regularly as much as you can.
Late morning	Lead the worship service.
Lunch	Have lunch with either leaders or second-time guests.
Afternoon	Make one-minute phone calls. Review worship service and sermon. Tend to administrative matters.
Late afternoon and evening	Relax!

APPENDIX ONE

THE AUTHOR

The material in this appendix is the work of JD Pearring. JD is the director of GHCNetwork, the church planting arm of Growing Healthy Churches. Under God's good hand and JD's leadership, GHC has been able to plant eighty new congregations from 2002 through 2010. These eighty new congregations are located in sixteen states. More than two thousand people have become new disciples of Jesus Christ as a result of the ministry of these new congregations. JD is a church planter magnet, attracting key leaders who follow God and commit themselves to the vision and mission of GHC and JD's leadership. I know of very few people who lead well and attract so many other leaders as JD Pearring. GHC is blessed by God to have JD sitting on our bus in the church reproduction seat.

THE MATERIAL

These few pages provide excellent and wise insight for pastors, whether they are leading established congregations or new church plants. It is biblical in its foundation and reflects wise insight into life, congregations, and pastoral leadership. I highly commend it to you for your reading. It is worth the investment of your time.

Paul D. Borden

COMMON LEADERSHIP ISSUES

JD PEARRING

Two of the most common issues that trip up church planters, pastors, and organizational directors are *leadership* and *agenda harmony*.

The leadership issue—who is really steering this ship—is especially difficult when the new "leader" joins an existing organization. Typically he or she is not the real leader at all.

In coaching on this issue, I ask the leaders I am working with to think of the people in any organization in terms of those older or younger than they are and those there before or after them. We coach by dividing the organization (or congregation) into four groups. The top left quadrant consists of those who are older than the newly appointed chief (pastor, boss, and so on) and were in the church or organization beforehand. The top right quadrant represents those who are younger than the new boss, but who were already in the organization. The bottom left quadrant shows those older than the director, but newer to the organization than the director. The bottom right quadrant signifies those younger than the boss and newer to the organization than the boss.

Older Before	Younger Before
Older After	Younger After

Which group is the most difficult to lead? The obvious answer is the top left quadrant—people who are older than the boss or pastor and are already in the organization. They tend to see the new pastor as merely a *chaplain.*

Chaplains are not empowered to lead.

I served as a chaplain for several professional baseball teams and was always reminded that I was not the leader—I was a hired hand employed to do their owners' bidding. My last chapel service came when I was helping an AA baseball team. Batting practice was over, and I steered a good group of the players into the dugout for a short service before the game. The PA system was blasting pregame music (fans had not been allowed inside the stadium yet). It was so loud that we couldn't conduct the chapel service. So I found the person in charge of the stadium sound—a kid, maybe sixteen years old. I asked him to turn down the music for chapel, and he gave me a look of disgust and a simple no. His point was obvious. As the kid in charge of pregame music, he outranked me as chaplain. I had to send the pitching coach to deal with the situation.

I never conducted a chapel service again. There is no leadership as a chaplain.

Which of the four groups is the next most difficult to lead?

It is the upper right quadrant: people who are younger than the new chief but were already in the organization when the new leader arrived. They tend to look at the new boss through the eyes of the older/before group. They typically regard the new director or pastor as an older *brother*, not as a leader.

I have two older brothers. Both are great guys, but I wouldn't follow them anywhere.

The next most difficult group to lead is the bottom right quadrant: people who are older than the person in charge, but newer to the organization. Since they are older, they don't naturally grant influence. They are inclined to look at the director as the *son or daughter* they wish they had.

Only the last group—those younger and newer than the pastor—naturally sees the pastor as a *leader*.

Older Before CHAPLAIN	Younger Before BROTHER/SISTER
Older After SON/DAUGHTER	Younger After LEADER

This diagram is a great tool for recruiting toward church planting. If a pastor takes a position in an established church, he or she immediately faces the two most difficult groups to lead. When thoughts of *why can't I get anything done around here?* arise, the obvious answer is "because you're not the leader."

Church planters confront the unfortunate task of starting with nothing. But people who join the organization will fall into the two easiest groups to lead, so planters can grow those groups.

A second issue tripping up directors is agenda harmony. Those in charge often expect everyone in the group to be on the same page, but that is rarely the case.

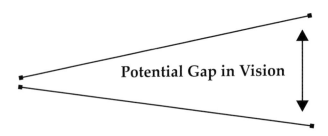

Potential Gap in Vision

At the beginning of a relationship, leaders and potential followers may feel that they are going in the same direction when they are actually moving away from each other.

For example, a church planter can explain to a prospect that the vision is for the church to use contemporary music. The prospect will often verbally assent, "Yes, I want contemporary music too!"

But over time, when the planter's vision gets fleshed out as loud, metallic, on-the-edge tunes, the prospect feels betrayed because his idea of contemporary is Bill Gaither.

A Lutheran pastor friend responded to this issue by revealing that on the previous Sunday he asked his music director to end their service with something more "up" than the usual sedate music. The music director smiled and told the pastor, "I got it!" That Sunday the church ended services with a rendition of "Do, Lord, Remember Me." Their signals were obviously crossed!

So, how can we help leaders close this agenda harmony gap? Divide people into four groups!

The upper left quadrant is comprised of people who like you as the leader, and they like the direction, the mission, the vision, and the values of the organization or the church. The upper right quadrant holds people who like you, but don't like the philosophy of the organization. It is not run how they would run things. The bottom left quadrant represents those who don't like you—they wouldn't choose you as a leader—but they do like where the organization is going. And the bottom right quadrant is made up of those wonderful people who don't like you or the organization.

Okay with you Okay with the church	Okay with you Not okay with the church
Not okay with you Okay with the church	Not okay with you Not okay with the church

In just about any organization you will find all four of these types of people.

So, how do you lead the different groups? What do you do with those who like you and the organization?

The simple answer is: don't mess it up! If you've been taking these people to lunch, keep it up! If you haven't been taking them to lunch, don't start—you might mess it up! Whatever you've been doing, keep doing.

How do you lead quadrant four—those who don't like you and don't like the church or organization?

The Apostle Paul had a strong suggestion for how to deal with these folks: "After a first and second warning, have nothing more to do with a person who causes conflict" (Titus 3:10). Paul said to outcounsel disgruntled members: warn them once, and then warn them a second time. After that, send them to the church down the street to mess it up and leave you alone!

I suspect that this is one of the most ignored commands in the Bible. We, as leaders, typically do everything but ask people to leave. We ignore this verse because implementing it is so difficult.

In the second church that I planted, a family emerged as "don't like me, don't like the direction" people. We were in a private worship prelaunch phase with about forty people (including kids—and pets!) on our launch team. I took this couple aside (they had three kids) and had a heart-to-heart talk about how this new church wasn't working for them. I encouraged them to find a church that would be better fit. With great relief, they hugged me and left. As they did, I did the math. I had just asked one-eighth of our church to leave—and these people tithed! (Doesn't it seem that a lot of "don't like you, don't like the church" people tithe?) I knew we'd just experienced addition by subtraction, but it hurt. It did help immensely in the long run, though.

How can we best lead those in the second quadrant, who like us but are not that wild about our vision?

An effective approach is to ask them to serve as short-term missionaries for a time. They may not like what we're doing, but we can ask them to do us a personal favor and serve for a time.

In our third church plant, an older couple—parents of our top associate—came to a few of our information meetings. It was clear that what we were envisioning didn't scratch where they itched. But I asked them to become involved. I admitted that they could find a comfortable church to sit and soak, or they could join this new venture, give us credibility with their presence as older folks, and serve as short-term missionaries. I acknowledged that it would be cross-cultural ministry for them, but the potential for them to impact younger families was immense. They took the challenge.

In our second plant we had asked a good number of folks from a nearby church to serve as short-term missionaries. We learned a lesson the hard way: remember to stagger the terms of service. When people finished their terms at the same time and went back to their home churches, we had more of a loss than if folks had trickled back.

Quadrant three: What do we do with folks who like the vision and mission of the organization, but don't necessarily like us as the leader? Believe it or not, there are people who won't immediately be drawn to you!

The best way to manage these folks is to connect them to another leader in the organization. Most pastors miss this point. We think everyone has to like us and be directly connected to us (this explains why the average church in the United States is comprised of about seventy-five people—about as many as one pastor can connect with personally). Find another leader that these folks can relate to, and let that relationship grow.

Okay with you Okay with the church Don't mess it up!	Okay with you Not okay with the church Ask to serve as short-term missionaries
Not okay with you Okay with the church Connect with another key leader	Not okay with you Not okay with the church Outcounsel.

The truth is that folks in quadrants two and three don't stay there very long. Those conflicted with liking the leader but not the vision or vice versa cannot stay in that conflict or on that bubble very long. They will move to the like/like quadrant or don't like/don't like area pretty swiftly.

This is one compelling reason to outcounsel the divisive people quickly. They can bring others down.

Billy Martin, the legendary baseball manager, used to say that in any baseball team there would be ten guys who would run through a wall for the manager; five guys who hated the manager's guts; and the other ten who were undecided. Martin warned that the number one job of the baseball manager, more important than making out a lineup or in-game strategy, was to keep the guys who hated you away from those who were undecided. He sternly advised that when making out roommate assignments (in his day, players shared hotel rooms on the road; now they all get suites), the manager should not put players who disliked him in the same room with those who hadn't decided yet.

Those who are undecided about the leadership and direction will soon move toward or away from the leader. And the amazing thing is we know what will cause them to move.

One factor will move folks from the middle to liking the leader and the vision or disliking both. We rarely talk about that factor in leadership, but it is critical. That factor is momentum.

Momentum will drive folks up or down. Positive momentum will cause those who like the leader, but are unsure about the vision, to jump on board because it is working. Positive momentum will cause those who like the direction, but have their doubts about the leader to say, "He's not that bad a guy," or "I guess she knows what she is doing."

Negative momentum will do the opposite. If things are not going well, those in quadrant two will conclude, "I really didn't like him or her all that much." And those in quadrant three will quip, "I told you he'd mess it up."

Momentum is critical to agenda harmony.

And the great news is that we, as leaders, get to manage the momentum of our ministries. Really. The leader is in charge of managing momentum.

There are three types of people: those who make things happen; those who watch things happen; and those who ask, "What the heck just happened?" Leaders are called to make things happen: "Don't hesitate to be enthusiastic—be on fire in the Spirit as you serve the Lord!" (Rom. 12:11). The Apostle Paul reminds us that we're to keep pushing momentum. When can we let up? "Never." When can we take our foot off the gas pedal? "Never." We're to keep that fervor. Too many pastors, too many who are in charge, sit back and wait when God says to keep pushing.

The great news is that Jesus promises positive momentum: "I'll build my church on this rock. The gates of the underworld won't be able to stand against it" (Matt. 16:18). Jesus promises that no matter what, his kingdom will have positive momentum. And as leaders we need to keep pushing that.

But how? Romans 12:12-13 explains how to keep the zeal, the fervor, the momentum:

"Be happy in your hope, stand your ground when you're in trouble, and devote yourselves to prayer. Contribute to the needs of God's people, and welcome strangers into your home."

There are three ways to keep momentum and ultimately harmony.

First, *be joyful in hope.* The leader's job is to constantly instill hope and joy by providing that next big thing. I've seen too many new churches lose momentum when after all their work for a launch or grand opening, they fail to highlight the next big thing. At the launch Sunday the next big thing needs to be promoted and advertised. At Easter we need to push the next big thing that is planned for right after Easter, and at that event, the next big thing needs to be unveiled.

Second, *be patient in affliction.* Amazingly Paul states that the way to zeal and fervor and momentum is to press through difficult times. Again, Jesus promises that nothing will prevail against his kingdom.

Great momentum can be built during tough times. Winston Churchill put it this way: "Success is going from failure to failure without loss of enthusiasm."

I mentioned the couple who took the challenge to serve as short-term missionaries in our third church plant. Even though they were older than our target group, they decided to join the launch team and get busy helping out. But a tragic thing happened on our launch day—Easter. The husband of this couple never woke up. He died in his sleep. When I arrived to help set up for services at the theater complex where our church was meeting, this man's son—our top associate pastor—was distraught. And his wife was wailing. Our associate said she could have been a professional mourner. It was an extremely difficult way to kick off a new church.

I drove back home and hopped in the shower again, asking God to somehow provide positive momentum in the midst of a negative situation. I went back to church and preached the launch message with the now very relevant conclusion that we are all set to die and we need to turn to Jesus for assurance of heaven. Then I announced that services for this launch team member would be held that Friday.

The funeral service amazed me. Just about everyone from our launch service showed up with food, drinks, and condolences. I thought, *Wow, God, you do bring positive momentum even in something tragic.* Our church had a sense of community in just five days that many churches don't get in five years—or ever. I've even thought that having a launch team member die is a great strategy in church planting—especially if you can pick who dies! Anyway, leaders can promote positive momentum even in affliction.

Third, *be faithful in prayer.* When a lot of people pray that something great will happen, usually something great will happen.

Conclusion: working through leadership clarity and achieving agenda harmony are two of the most common and recurring issues faced by pastors and organizational directors. It takes exceptional leadership skills to handle these issues, but understanding the types of people we are dealing with can make a big difference in ensuring success.

APPENDIX TWO

MEAL MEETINGS, MONEY, AND WAISTLINES

In this book I recommend using meals, particularly breakfasts and lunches, as times to conduct ministry. I also discuss visitor lunches on Sunday with second- and third-time guests. This is often a foreign concept to lay leaders in smaller congregations, particularly if the congregations are not doing well financially and are in smaller and more rural communities. I want to discuss how the pastor needs to handle these situations.

Beginning with preliminary meetings with congregational leaders before being called or assigned to that congregation by a denominational leader, the pastor needs to lay out the strategy. The pastor needs to demonstrate that he or she has been called to lead systemic change in order to help any congregation the pastor serves to become obedient in fulfilling the Great Commission. The pastor understands that such work is challenging and that as the pastor, he or she assumes a typical workweek will involve a minimum of fifty hours. In addition the pastor recognizes the need to be in the community as often as the study or church office. The pastor shares that she or he will spend much of the time with three kinds of people. The first group includes leaders and future leaders within the congregation. The pastor states that congregations grow as both leaders and groups are multiplied. The second group includes people in the community who have positions of influence in government, educational, business, and nonprofit enterprises. These meetings are to help the congregation eventually serve the community well and become a respected and integral member of the community in order to be an excellent testimony for Jesus Christ. The third group includes people in the community who are not yet disciples of Jesus Christ; the pastor wants to develop relationships with them in order to eventually introduce them to a personal relationship with Jesus Christ.

Meeting many individuals and developing relationships with them take time. The pastor will need to meet many of these people on their turf or in neutral places like restaurants and coffee shops. Also, the pastor wants to maximize his or her schedule to ensure that the congregation and its needs are met, and the best way to do this is to constantly have a series of meetings over meals. Since most pastors in smaller situations, as well as larger situations, are not paid well, money needs to be freed up for these expenses. The pastor needs to promise that congregational leaders will be apprised of how the pastor's goals and strategies are being met and that the pastor will be careful with the funds in order to keep costs to a minimum. The pastor makes a case to the leaders that these dollars are an investment, not an expense, in the future of the congregation. The pastor might have already looked at the congregation's budget, assuming there is little in it for such expenses, and suggested line items that can be changed free up dollars that have already been allocated.

The pastor should provide examples of how costs will be conserved without spending large sums of money. For example, breakfast may be coffee and a bagel. Or the pastor may meet with some in the park over a brown bag lunch. Other times, people in the congregation may meet in the pastor's office, and each person brings a lunch. Obviously with some people in the community, the pastor may want to take them to a restaurant where they can be served a meal. Perhaps a special room could be set aside in the church facility, where the invited guest and pastor are served "room service" presented by someone in the congregation committed to helping the pastor have strategic meals for the kingdom.

The main point is that meals from the pastor's perspective are to make great use and take advantage of the time and setting to lead. Many people are much more open and will participate more fully in a conversation when they are eating and drinking during a meal.

Boards and councils may not agree to whatever the pastor asks. This response tells the pastor a lot about the situation at this congregation. The pastor may need to go to plan B or even C. One option is to seek out people in the congregation with financial means who want to see change and ask if they will provide funds for implementing this strategy. The pastor may need to locate a suitable place to eat that is quite inexpensive and take people there only when it would be rude and improper to ask them to bring their own lunch. Meanwhile the pastor can meet others over meals where each person provides his or her own. Wise leaders will figure out how to resolve the issue and in some cases make it happen with their own funds if they believe the strategy is crucial.

Another issue is the pastor's health and dietary restrictions. Intentional planning and discipline can address this issue. Pastors can eat the appropriate foods on their way to a meal and simply order water and soup or salad. If the pastor is bringing lunch, that lunch can be prepared to meet dietary needs about which the pastor is concerned. Again, leaders figure out how to complete the job despite barriers or obstructions.

The purposes behind this strategy are about meeting people outside the congregation and developing leaders within it; being seen in the community and meeting the right people in the community who can help the pastor lead the congregation to achieve the mission and vision; and not wasting time that can be used for other agendas of the pastor that lead to change. It is not about eating out; it is about developing relationships that help produce systemic change through the strategy of hospitality.